D1784865

Epicurus

A E. 1869-1945 Taylor

Nabu Public Domain Reprints:

You are holding a reproduction of an original work published before 1923 that is in the public domain in the United States of America, and possibly other countries. You may freely copy and distribute this work as no entity (individual or corporate) has a copyright on the body of the work. This book may contain prior copyright references, and library stamps (as most of these works were scanned from library copies). These have been scanned and retained as part of the historical artifact.

This book may have occasional imperfections such as missing or blurred pages, poor pictures, errant marks, etc. that were either part of the original artifact, or were introduced by the scanning process. We believe this work is culturally important, and despite the imperfections, have elected to bring it back into print as part of our continuing commitment to the preservation of printed works worldwide. We appreciate your understanding of the imperfections in the preservation process, and hope you enjoy this valuable book.

CONTENTS

FOREWORD

THIS little volume is, as its title proclaims, a brief study of the thought and temperament of a remarkable man, not the history of a scientific school. The band of comrades who gathered round Epicurus in his Garden were held together not so much by a common intellectual interest in the pursuit of truth as by the ties of personal affection among themselves and personal devotion to a master whom they regarded more as a Redeemer from the ills of life than as a mere thinker. That the feelings of the Epicurean society of a later date were of the same kind is amply proved by the tone of the poem of Lucretius. Atomism as a scientific hypothesis owes nothing to Epicurus or to any of his followers; he found it already in existence, and every innovation which he made upon its existing form was, from the scientific point of view, a change for the worse. As a man of science, his place is with the circle-squarers and the earth-flatteners. This, together with the fact that a volume on ancient Atomism is announced to appear in due time in the present series, will explain why I have said no more about the really scientific Atomism of the fifth century B.C. than was absolutely necessary to place the indifference of Epicurus and his followers to science in the proper light. For similar reasons I

EPICURUS

have avoided dealing with Lucretius, the one man
of genius in the Epicurean following, except where
it has been necessary to cite him as a mere witness to
the Epicurean tradition. The one point of interest
to the student of the history of physical theories
which has, as I hope, been made clearer than is usual
in works on ancient Atomism is that the Epicurean
Physics are throughout the result of an unhappy
attempt, which no clear-headed thinker would ever
have undertaken, to fuse together the radically incompatible doctrines of Democritus and Aristotle.
If the establishment of this important point has made
my second chapter into something like the exposure
of a charlatan, the fault is not mine. For a different
reason I have said little as to the few facts definitely
known about the illustrious obscurities of the Epicurean succession. I trust some compensation may
be found in the chapter on the anti-Epicurean polemic
carried on by the Platonic Academy.

The volume has been throughout written from the
original sources with little use of any modern works
on Epicurus, except, of course, Usener's invaluable
collection of his extant writings and fragments, and
Koerte's compilation of the fragments of Metrodorus.
I trust that my treatment in this way may have
gained in freshness something of what it has, no
doubt, lost in erudition.

A. E. TAYLOR.

St. Andrew   July 1910.

EPICURUS

CHAPTER I

THE LIFE OF EPICURUS

WHEN we turn from Plato and Aristotle, the great constructive thinkers of the fourth century before Christ, to the study of the new sects or schools,—that of Epicurus was, in date of foundation, slightly older than the others,—which came into being early in the third century, under the successors of Alexander, we feel at first as if we had passed into a new moral atmosphere.

Philosophy seems to have dwindled from the magnificent attempt to arrive at scientific knowledge of God, man, and nature into a mere theory of conduct, and, in the theory of conduct itself, the old conception of the individual man as essentially a member of a community freely banded together to live the 'good life,' in virtue of which Plato and Aristotle could treat what we call 'ethics' as a mere part of the wider study of society, its aims and institutions 'Politics', to have

A   I

given place to a purely individualistic doctrine of morals which has lost the sense of the inseparable union of the civilised man with the civilised society. So keenly has this difference of tone been felt that writers on philosophy have almost always adopted the death of Aristotle as one of those historical land-marks which indicate the ending of an old era, and the beginning of a new, like the English Revolution of 1688 or the French Revolution of 1789. The cause of so great a change has been variously sought in the special conditions of life in the third century. Under the hard pressure of the Macedonian dynasts, it has been said, Philosophy naturally became identical with the theory of conduct, because, in such untoward times, the effort to understand the world had to be abandoned for the task of making life bearable. The theory of statesmanship shrank into a mere doctrine of morals because with the battle of Chaeronea the free life of the independent city-states came once for all to an end. Others, again, have seen the key to the developments of Philosophy in the third century in a return of Greek thought from the 'idealism' of Plato and Aristotle into the materialism, which, as is alleged, was natural to it. There is an element of truth in these views, but they are none the less, as they stand, thoroughly unhistorical.

It is true, to be sure, that under the Macedonian rulers the ordinary man was cut loose from the immediate participation in public affairs of moment which had been characteristic of the life of the sovereign city-state, and that individualism in ethics is the natural counterpart of cosmopolitanism in public life. It is also true that both the Epicurean and the Stoic systems regarded the theory of the chief good for man and the right rule of life as the culminating achievement of Philosophy, and that both tended, in their doctrine of nature, to revert to views which are curiously reactionary as compared with those of Plato and Aristotle. But it is false to suppose that the death of Aristotle or the appearance of Epicurus as a teacher really marks any solution of historical continuity. From the time of Pythagoras at least Philosophy had always been to the Greek mind what personal religion is to ourselves, a 'way of life,' that is a means to the salvation of the soul, and this conception is no less prominent in Plato and Aristotle, when they are rightly read, than in Epicurus and Zeno. And, with regard to the alleged effects on Philosophy of the disappearance of the old life of the free city-state, it is important to recollect that Aristotle composed his *Politics* under the Macedonian régime, and that the Athens of Pericles had ceased to exist, except as a mere shadow of its former past, before Plato wrote the *Republic*. If any single date can be taken as signalising the end of the old order, it should rather be that of the surrender of Athens to Lysander, or even that of the defeat of Nicias before Syracuse, than that of the collapse of the anti-Macedonian agitation of Demosthenes and Hypereides on the field of Chaeronea.[1]

Similarly the cosmopolitanism and individualism of the Epicurean and Stoic ethics is no new departure, nor even a reaction to the attitude of the 'Sophists' of the fifth century, but a direct continuance of traditions which had never died out. Epicurus is directly connected by a series of discernible though little known predecessors with Democritus, just as Zeno is with Antisthenes and Diogenes. Nor is it true that the third century was a period of intellectual stagnation. It is the age of the foundation of the great Museum and Library at Alexandria, of the development of literary criticism into a craft, of the creation of the organised and systematic study of history and chronology, and the compilation of full and exact observations of natural history in the widest sense of the term. Above all, it is the time to which belong the greatest of the Greek mathematicians, and astronomers, Eudoxus, Euclid, Eratosthenes, Aristarchus of Samos, Apollonius of Perga, Archimedes.

The notion that a century so full of original scientific work was one of intellectual sterility is probably due

[1] The conception of Chaeronea as *par excellence* the 'bad victory, fatal to liberty' comes in the end from Plutarch to whom it was natural as a Boeotian. Boeotia's hour of glory,— the brief and brilliant career of Epameinondas,—belonged to the fourth century, and her political importance ceased for ever with the annihilation of the 'sacred band' at Chaeronea. For Greece at large the Macedonian victory had much less signif.came

to a simple historical accident. For the most part the writings of the successors of Plato and Aristotle, as well as those of the early Stoics, happen not to have been preserved to us. Hence we readily tend to forget that the scientific and philosophical work of the Academy and Lyceum was vigorously propagated all through the period in which the new schools were seeking to establish themselves, and that the Stoics, the most important of the new sects, were not merely keenly interested in 'Physics,' but were also devoted to minute researches into Formal Logic, much of which, in the shape in which the Middle Ages have handed it down to us, has been inherited directly from them. Hence we come to look on the indifference to logic and scientific Physics which was characteristic of the temperament of Epicurus as if it was a universal feature of 'Post-Aristotelian' thought, and falsely ascribe to the age what is really true of the man. Of the age it would be much more true to say that it was one of devotion to the advancement of special sciences rather than to the elaboration of fresh general points of view in Philosophy. In this respect it is closely parallel with the middle of our own nineteenth century, when the interest in philosophical speculation which had culminated in the 'absolute Philosophy' of Hegel gave place to absorption in the empirical study of Nature and History.

Having said so much to guard ourselves against a common misunderstanding we may proceed to consider what is known of the personal life and habits of Epicurus. Our chief source of information is the so-called *Life of Epicurus* which forms the last section of the ill-digested scrap-book known as the *Lives of the Philosophers* by Laertius Diogenes.[1] (Of additional matter from other sources we have little beyond one or two unimportant letters of Epicurus himself which have been preserved, along with much later Epicurean materials, under the lava which overwhelmed the city of Herculaneum). In its present form the work of Diogenes only dates from the middle of the third century A.D., and, indeed, hardly deserves to be called a 'work' at all, since it can be shown to contain notes which must have been made by generations of successive readers, and seems never to have been subjected to the final revision of a single editor. Its value, for us, depends on the fact that it is largely made up of notices drawn from much more ancient authorities who are often quoted by name. This is particularly the case with the *Life* of Epicurus which is, in the main, drawn from the statements of Epicurus himself, his intimate friends, and his contemporary opponents.

---

[1] The view of Cobet followed in my *Plato* in the present series, that 'Laertius Diogenes' means Diogenes *of Laerte*, is mistaken. The double name is a mere instance of the fashion, current among the Greek-speaking citizens of the Roman Empire, in the third century A.D., of copying the Roman practice, according to which a man had, besides his personal name (praenomen), a second name (nomen) indicating his *gens* or clan, *e.g.* Gnaeus Pompeius, Titus Livius, Gaius Manlius, Marcus Antonius.

and may thus be taken as, on the whole, a fair representation of what was known or inferred about him by the Alexandrian writers of 'Successions,' or Handbooks to the history of Philosophy, the earliest of whom date from the latter part of the third century B.C. For this reason, and for the sake of giving the reader a specimen of the biographical material available in the study of ancient Philosophy in a specially favourable case, I proceed to give a complete rendering of the strictly biographical part of Diogenes' account of Epicurus from the text of Usener.

'Epicurus, an Athenian, son of Neocles and Chaerestrata, of the township of Gargettus, and of the house of the Philaidae,[1] according to Metrodorus in his work *On Good Birth*. Heracleides, in the *Epitome of Sotion*, and others say that he was brought up in Samos, where the Athenians had made a plantation, and only came to Athens at the age of eighteen when Xenocrates was conducting his school in the Academy and Aristotle at Chalcis (*i.e.* 323/2 B.C.). After the death of Alexander of Macedon and the expulsion of the Athenians by Perdiccas, he followed his father (they say) to Colophon. He spent some while there and gathered disciples round him, and then returned to Athens in the year of Anaxicrates. For a time he pursued Philosophy in association with others; after-

---

[1] The Philaidae were a well-known house of old-established nobility with a legendary pedigree going back to Ajax and Aeacus.

wards he established the special sect called by his name and appeared on his own account. He says himself that he first touched Philosophy at the age of fourteen. But Apollodorus the Epicurean says in Bk. I. of his *Life of Epicurus,* that he was led to Philosophy by dissatisfaction with his schoolmasters who had failed to explain to him Hesiod's lines about Chaos. Hermippus says that he had been an elementary schoolmaster himself but afterwards fell in with the books of Democritus and threw himself at once into Philosophy, and that this is why Timon says of him :—

> From the island of Samos the loudest and last
> Of the swaggering scientists came ;
> 'Twas a dominie's brat whose defects in *bon ton*
> Might have put the creation to shame.

His brothers, too, were converted by him and followed his Philosophy. There were three of them, and their names were Neocles, Charidemus, and Aristobulus, as we are told by Philodemus the Epicurean in his *Compendium of Philosophers,* Bk. X. Another associate was a slave of his called Mys, as Myronianus says in his *Summary of Historical Parallels.* Diotimus the Stoic, who hated him, has calumniated him savagely by producing fifty lewd letters as the work of Epicurus. So has he who collected under the name of Epicurus the correspondence ascribed to Chrysippus. Other calumniators are Poseidonius the Stoic, Nicolaus and Sotion in the twelve books entitled

THE LIFE OF EPICURUS

An Answer to Diocles, which deal with the observance of the twentieth day of the month,[1] and Dionysius of Halicarnassus. They actually say that he used to accompany his mother on her rounds into cottages, and recite her spells for her, and that he helped his father to teach children their letters for a miserable pittance. Nay, that he played the pimp to one of his brothers, and kept Leontion the courtesan. That he gave out as his own the atomic theory of Democritus and the Hedonism of Aristippus. That he was not a true born Athenian citizen, as we learn from Timocrates and the work on *The Early Years of Epicurus* by Herodotus. That he heaped shameful adulation on Mithres the intendant of Lysimachus, addressing him in correspondence as Gracious Preserver, and My very good Lord. Nay, he even bestowed the same sycophantic flatteries on Idomeneus, on Herodotus, and on Timocrates, who exposed his secret abominations. In his correspondence he writes to Leontion, 'Gracious God, darling Leontion, how your sweet letter set me clapping and cheering when I read it'; and to Themista, the wife of Leonteus, 'If you do not both pay me a visit, I shall prove a very stone of Sisyphus to roll at a push wherever you and Themista invite me'; and to Pythocles, then in the bloom of his youth, 'Here I shall sit

---

[1] The twentieth of each month was a regular school holiday. Epicurus enjoined in his will that the day (as well as his birthday) should be celebrated as a feast in honour of himself by all his follower-.

awaiting your delightful and divine advent.' In another letter to Themista, according to Theodorus in Bk. IV. of his work *Against Epicurus*, he calls her 'Queen and huntress chaste and fair.'[1]

He corresponded, they allege, with a host of courtesans, particularly with Leontion, with whom Metrodorus also fell in love. Further, in the work *On the Moral End*, he writes: 'For my part I can form no notion of the good if I am to leave out the pleasures of taste and sex, of hearing and of form.' And (they say) in the letter to Pythocles he writes, 'For God's sake, crowd on sail and away from all "culture"!' Epictetus calls him a lewd writer and reviles him in round terms. Nay, worse, Timocrates, the brother of Metrodorus, a disciple who had deserted the School, says in his *Paradise of Delights* that Epicurus used to vomit twice a day in consequence of his riotous living, and that he himself escaped by the skin of his teeth from the 'midnight lore' and 'mystical fellowship.' Further, that Epicurus was grossly ignorant of science and even more ignorant of the art of life; that he fell into so pitiable a habit of body as not to be able to rise from his litter for years on end; that he spent a mina a day on his table, as he writes himself to Leontion and

---

[1] The text here is purely conjectural. My rendering follows Usener's suggestion, according to which the scandal consisted in applying to Themista an epithet (ἀριάγνη, 'most virginal') which could only be used properly of a maiden goddess, and specially of Artemis the virgin huntress and protector of maidens.

to the philosophers at Mytilene. That he and Metrodorus enjoyed the favours of Mammarion, Hedeia, Erotion, Nicidion [1] and other courtesans. That in the thirty-seven books of his treatise on *Nature* he is nearly always repeating himself and transcribing the ideas of others, especially of Nausiphanes, and says in so many words, 'But enough of this; the fellow's mouth was always in labour with some piece of sophistic bragadoccio, like those of so many others of the slaves.' And Epicurus is charged with having said himself of Nausiphanes in his letters, 'this threw him into such a passion that he started a personal polemic against me, and had the face to call me his scholar.' Indeed he used to call Nausiphanes a 'mollusc,' a 'boor,' a 'quack,' and a 'strumpet.' The Platonists he called 'Dionysius' lickspittles,' and Plato himself 'that thing of gold.' Aristotle, he said, was a rake who ran through his patrimony and then turned mountebank [2] and druggist. Protagoras was styled 'the Porter' and 'Democritus' scrivener,' and reproached with being a village dominie. Heraclitus he called 'the Muddler,' Democritus 'Dumb-ocritus,' Antidorus 'Zany-dorus,' the Cynics 'the national enemy,' the dialecticians 'a general pest,' Pyrrho 'Block' and 'Boor.' [3]

[1] The form of the names stamps the ladies in question as 'demi-mondaines.' We might venture on translating Leontion and Nicidion, with Wallace, by Léonie and Victorine. For the other three names try Maimie, Chérisette, and Désirée.

[2] Following the reading suggested by Usener.

[3] I have done my best to reproduce the effect of these abusive

Now all this is stark madness. There are abundant witnesses to his unsurpassed goodwill to all mankind: his native city, which honoured him with statues of bronze; his friends, who were too numerous to be reckoned by whole cities; his followers, who were all held spellbound by the charms of his doctrine—except Metrodorus of Stratonice, who deserted to Carneades, perhaps because he was depressed by his master's un-rivalled merits;[1] his school, which has maintained an unbroken existence, though almost all others have had their seasons of eclipse, and has been under a succession of innumerable heads, all of them faithful to the persuasion; his gratitude to his parents, beneficence to his brothers, and the humanity to his servants

distortions of names and vulgar epithets. Heracleitus is called a 'Muddler,' because he held that everything is changing into something else, and so, in his own phrase, looks on the world as a great *olla podrida*. Democritus was called Lerocritus because all he said was λῆρος, 'bosh.' So we may render by Dumb-ocritus, with the insinuation that no word of sense ever came from his mouth. The 'dialecticians' will be the formal logicians of the Megaric school, Stilpo and Diodorus and their associates, or possibly Zeno of Cittium, the founder of Stoicism.

[1] This sentence gives a good illustration of the way in which 'Diogenes' has been put together. As the words stand, the 'master' deserted by Metrodorus of Stratonice cannot gram-matically be other than Epicurus. This is historically absurd, since Carneades belongs to a time a full century later than Epicurus. It is manifest that we have here incorporated with the text a note on the defection of Metrodorus, in which mention was made of the merits of his immediate 'master,' the head of the Epicurean school in the time of Carneades.

which may be seen from his will, and from the fact that they shared in his Philosophy, the most notable of them being the aforesaid Mys; in a word, his universal benevolence. As for his piety towards the gods and his native land, words cannot describe them. 'Twas from excess of conscientiousness that he would not so much as touch political life. Consider, too, that though Hellas had then been overtaken by most troublous times, he spent his whole life at home, except that he made one or two flying visits to Ionia to see his friends in that quarter, who, in their turn, flocked from all parts to share the life in his Garden, as we are told particularly by Apollodorus, who adds that he payed eighty minae for the site. The life they led there, so says Diocles in Bk. III. of his *Brief Relation*, was of the simplest and plainest. They were amply content, so he says, with half a pint of *vin ordinaire*; their regular drink was water. Epicurus, he says, disapproved of the community of goods sanctioned by the saying of Pythagoras, 'what belongs to friends is common.' Such a system, he thought, implies distrust, and where there is distrust there can be no true friendship. He says himself in his letters that he can be satisfied with water and coarse bread. And again, 'Pray send me part of a pot of cheese, that I may be able to enjoy a varied table when I am in the mind.' Such was the character of the man who made 'Pleasure the end' an article of his creed. So Athenaeus celebrates him in the following epigram :—.

EPICURUS

Alas, we toil for nought ; the woful seed
Of strife and wars is man's insatiate greed :
True riches harbour in a little space,
Blind Fancy labours in an endless chase ;
This truth Neocles' deep-considering son
From heavenly Muse or Pytho's tripod won.

We shall see the truth of this still better, as we proceed, from his own writings and sayings.

Among the ancients, says Diocles, his preference was for Anaxagoras, though he controverted him on some points, and for Archelaus the teacher of Socrates. He says further that he trained his followers to learn his compositions by heart. Apollodorus says in his *Chronology* that he had heard Nausiphanes and Praxiphanes, but he himself denies it in his letter to Eurylochus, where he says he had no master but himself. He even declares (and Hermarchus agrees with him), that there never was any such philosopher as Leucippus[1] whom Apollodorus the Epicurean and others speak of as the teacher of Democritus. Demetrius of Magnesia adds that Epicurus had heard Xenocrates.

His style is plain and matter of fact, and is censured by the grammarian Aristophanes as very tame. But he was so lucid that in his *Rhetoric* he insists on no stylistic quality but lucidity. In correspondence he used 'Fare-well' and 'Live worthily' in place of the customary formula of salutation.

[1] On this assertion one can only remark in the language of Dr. Johnson, that 'If Epicurus said that, Epicurus lied.'

THE LIFE OF EPICURUS

Antigonus says in his *Life of Epicurus* that he copied his *Canon* from the *Tripod* of Nausiphanes, and that he had heard not only Nausiphanes but Pamphilus the Platonist in Samos. That he began Philosophy at the age of twelve, and became head of his school at thirty-two.

According to the *Chronology* of Apollodorus he was born in Olympiad 109/3, in the archonship of Sosigenes, on the 7th of Gamelion, seven years after Plato's death. That he first collected a school in Mytilene and Lampsacus at the age of thirty-two. This lasted for five years, at the end of which he migrated, as said, to Athens. His death fell in Olympiad 127/2, in the year of Pytharatus, at the age of seventy-two. He was followed as head of the School by Hermarchus of Mytilene, son of Agemortus. The cause of death was strangury due to calculus, as Hermarchus, too, says in his correspondence. The fatal illness lasted a fortnight. Hermarchus further relates that he entered a brazen bath filled with hot water, called for some neat wine which he took off at a draught, enjoined his friends not to forget his doctrines, and so came to his end. I have composed the following lines upon him :—

> Farewell, my friends ; be mindful of my lore ;
> Thus Epicurus spoke,—and was no more :
> Hot was the bath, and hot the bowl he quaffed ;
> Chill Hades followed on the after-draught.[1]

Such then was the tenour of his life, and the manner

[1] Sad doggerel—but not more so than the original.

of his end. His will runs as follows. [The main provisions are that the 'Garden and its appurtenances' are to be held in trust for the successors of Epicurus, and their associates. A house in the suburb Melite is to be inhabited by Hermarchus and his disciples for the former's lifetime. Provision is made for the due performance of the ritual for the dead in memory of the parents and brethren of Epicurus, for the regular keeping of his birthday, for the regular festival of the twentieth of each month, and for annual commemoration of his brothers and his friend Polyaenus. The son of Metrodorus and the son of Polyaenus are to be under the guardianship of the trustees on condition that they live with Hermarchus and share his Philosophy. The daughter of Metrodorus is to receive a dowry out of the estate on condition that she behaves well and marries with the approval of Hermarchus. Provision is to be made for an aged and needy member of the community. The 'books' of Epicurus, *i.e.* presumably the manuscripts of his works, are bequeathed to Hermarchus. If Hermarchus should die before the children of Metrodorus come of age, they are to be under the guardianship of the trustees. Mys and three other slaves are to receive their freedom.]

The following lines were written to Idomeneus on the very point of death : 'I write these lines to you and your friends as I bring to a close the last happy day of my life. I am troubled with strangury and dysentery in unsurpassable degree, but I can confront

it all with a joy of mind due to remembrance of
our past discussions. To you I leave the injunction to
take care of the children of Metrodorus as befits your
lifelong association with me and Philosophy.'

'He had numerous disciples. Specially distinguished
were Metrodorus of Lampsacus, son of Athenaeus,
(or Timocrates) and Sande, who never left him after
making his acquaintance except for one six months' visit
to his birthplace, whence he returned to him. He was
an excellent man in all respects, as is attested by
Epicurus himself in sundry Dedications and in the
Timocrates, Bk. III. With all these excellences he
bestowed his sister Batis on Idomeneus, and took
Leontion the Athenian courtesan under his protection
as a morganatic wife. He was imperturbable in the
face of troubles and death, as Epicurus says in his
Metrodorus, Bk. I. They say he died in his fifty-third
year, seven years before Epicurus. Epicurus himself
implies that he had predeceased him by the injunction in the aforesaid will to care for his children.
Another was the aforesaid Timocrates, a worthless
brother of Metrodorus. [Here follows a list of the
works of M.]

'Another was Polyaenus of Lampsacus, son of
Athenodorus, according to Philodemus an upright
and amiable man. Also Hermarchus of Mytilene, son
of Agemortus, who succeeded to the headship of the
school. He was born of poor parents, and originally
a teacher of rhetoric by profession. The following

admirable works are ascribed to him. [The list follows.] He was an able man and died of a palsy.

'*Item*, Leonteus of Lampsacus and his wife Themista, the same with whom Epicurus corresponded. *Item*, Colotes and Idomeneus, both of Lampsacus. These are the most eminent names. We must include Polystratus who followed Hermarchus, and was succeeded by Dionysius, and he by Basileides. Apollodorus, the 'despot of the Garden,' who composed over four hundred books, is also a man of note. Then there are the two Ptolemies of Alexandria, the dark and the fair; Zeno of Sidon, a pupil of Apollodorus and a prolific author; Demetrius, surnamed the Laconic; Diogenes of Tarsus, the author of the *Selected Essays*; Orion; and some others whom the genuine Epicureans decry as Sophists.

'There were also three other persons of the name Epicurus: (1) the son of Leonteus and Themista, (2) an Epicurus of Magnesia, (3) a *maître d'armes*. Epicurus was a most prolific author.' [Follows a list of his works, and the writer then proceeds to give a summary of his doctrine.]'

The preceding pages have given us a fairly full account of the life and personality of Epicurus as known to the students of antiquity. I may supplement it with a few remarks intended to make the chronology clear, and to call attention to one or two of the salient points in the character which it discloses to us.

First as to chronology. Of the authorities used in

the *Life* far the best is Apollodorus, whose versified *Chronology* embodied the results of the great Eratosthenes. His data make it clear that Epicurus was born on the 7th of Gamelion (*i.e.* in our January) 341 B.C., and died in 270 B.C. They also enable us to fix his first appearance as an independent teacher in Mytilene and the neighbourhood, approximately in 310, and his removal to Athens in 306/5 B.C. We may take it also as certain, from other sources as well as from the evidence of Timon, that the place of Epicurus' birth was the island of Samos, where a colony or plantation was established by the Athenians in the year 352/1, Neocles, the father of Epicurus, being, as we learn from Strabo, one of the settlers. When the Athenians were expelled from Samos by the regent Perdiccas in 322, Neocles for unknown reasons preferred emigrating to the Ionian town of Colophon to returning to Athens, and Epicurus followed him. The assertion of his enemies that he was no true Athenian citizen (this would be *their* way of explaining his lifelong abstention from public affairs), may have no better foundation than the fact of his birth at a distance from Athens, or, again, may be explained by supposing that Neocles had some special connection with the Ionic cities of the Asiatic coast. In any case the salient points to take note of are that Epicurus must have received his early education in Samos (itself an Ionian island), and that his philosophical position had been definitely settled before he left Asia Minor to establish himself at Athens. This will account for the attitude of aloofness steadily maintained by the society of the 'Garden' towards the great indigenous Athenian philosophical institutions, and also for the marked Ionicisms of Epicurus' technical terminology. It is clear from the narratives preserved by Diogenes that the family of Neocles was in straitened circumstances, but there is no more ground to take the polemical representation of Neocles and his wife as a hedge dominie and village sorceress seriously than there is to believe the calumnies of Demosthenes on the parents of Aeschines. That Neocles was an elementary schoolmaster may, however, be true, since it is asserted by the satirist Timon, who belongs to the generation immediately after Epicurus, and the schoolmaster, as we see from the *Mimes* of Herodas, was not a person of much consideration in the third century. With regard to the date of the establishment of Epicurus at Athens one should note, by way of correcting erroneous impressions about 'Post-Aristotelian Philosophy,' that when Epicurus made his appearance in the city which was still the centre of Greek intellectual activity, Theophrastus, the immediate successor of Aristotle, had not completed half of his thirty-four years' presidency over the Peripatetic school, and Xenocrates, the third head of the Academy, and an immediate pupil of Plato, had only been dead some eight years. The illusion by which we often think of the older schools as having run their course before Epicurus came to the front may be easily dispelled by the recollection that Epicurus's chief disciples, Metrodorus, Hermarchus, Colotes, all wrote special attacks on various Platonic dialogues, and that Hermarchus moreover wrote a polemic against Aristotle and Epicurus himself one against Theophrastus, while, as we shall see later, we still possess a 'discourse of Socrates' in which an anonymous member of the Academy sharply criticises Epicurus as the author of superficial doctrines which are just coming into vogue with the half-educated.

With regard to the personal character of Epicurus one or two interesting things stand out very clearly from the conflicting accounts of admirers like the original writer of the main narrative which figures in Diogenes, and again Lucretius, and enemies, like the detractors mentioned by Diogenes, or unfriendly critics like Plutarch and his Academic authorities. We may disregard altogether the representation of Epicurus and his associates as sensualists who ruined their constitutions by debauchery. There is abundant testimony, not solely from Epicurean sources, for the simplicity of the life led in the Garden, not to say that most of the calumnious stories are discredited by the fact that the worst of them were told by personal or professional enemies like Timocrates, the Judas of the society, and the Stoic philosopher who palmed off a fictitious 'lewd correspondence' on the world under the name of Epicurus. Abuse of this kind was a regular feature

of controversy, and deserves just as much credit as
the accusations of secret abominations which Demosthenes and Aeschines flung at each other, that is to
say, none at all. What we do see clearly is that
Epicurus was personally a man of clinging and winning
temperament, quick to gain friendship and steadfast in
keeping it. There is something of a feminine winsome-
ness about his solicitude for the well-being of his
friends and their children, and the extravagant gratitude which the high-flown phrases quoted from his
letters show for the minor offices of friendship. At
the same time Epicurus and his 'set' exhibit the
weaknesses natural to a temperament of this kind.
Their horror of the anxieties and burdens of family
life, their exaggerated estimate of the misery which
is caused in human life by fear of death and the
possibilities of a life to come—matters with which we
shall find ourselves closely concerned in later chapters,
—testify to a constitutional timidity and a lack of
moral robustness. The air of the Garden is, to say
the least of it, morally relaxing; one feels in reading
the remains of Epicurus and Metrodorus that one is
dealing with moral invalids, and that Nietzsche was
not far from the truth when he spoke of Epicurus as
the first good example in history of a 'decadent.'
Partly we may explain the fact by the well-attested
physical invalidism of the founders of the school.
Epicurus, as we see from Diogenes, though he lived
to a decent age, was for years in feeble health, and it

is significant that Metrodorus and Colotes, two of his
chief disciples, died before him at a comparatively
early age.   We shall probably find the key at once to
the Epicurean insistence on the life of simple and
homely fare, and to the violence with which, as we
shall see, he and his friends insisted on the value of
the 'pleasures of the belly,' to the great scandal of
their later critics, in the assumption that they were
life-long dyspeptics.   (The ancients simply inverted
the order of causation when they observed that the
bad health of Epicurus and Metrodorus might be
regarded as God's judgment on the impiety of their
tenets.)

The ugliest feature in the character of Epicurus, as
revealed in his life and remains, is his inexcusable
ingratitude to his teachers, and his wholesale abuse
of all the thinkers who had gone before him.   This
tone of systematic detraction was taken up by his
friends; the quotations given in Plutarch's Essay
against Colotes are a perfect mine of scurrilities
directed against every eminent thinker of the past or
the present who had in any way strayed from the
path of rigid orthodoxy as understood by Epicurus.
There can be no doubt that the object of all this
abuse was to make Epicurus appear, as he claimed to
be, no man's pupil but his own, the one and only
revealer of the way of salvation.   And yet it is quite
clear, as we shall see, that Epicurus is in every way
the least independent of the philosophers of antiquity.

EPICURUS

There is no reason to doubt that he had originally been instructed in Samos by a member of the Platonic school, and the bitterness with which the Academy afterwards attacked his character and doctrines may, as has been suggested, have been partly due to the sense that he was, in some sort, an apostate from the fold. His treatment of the teachers from whom he had learned the Atomism which has come to be thought of as his characteristic doctrine is absolutely without excuse.

We shall see in the next chapter that the whole doctrine is a blundering perversion of the really scientific Atomism of a much greater man, Democritus, and that Epicurus had undoubtedly derived his knowledge of the doctrine from Nausiphanes, a philosopher whose importance we are only now beginning to learn from the Herculaneum papyri. Yet both Democritus and Nausiphanes are, on the showing of Epicurus' own admirers, covered by him with the coarsest abuse, and one may even suspect that we have to thank Epicurean anxiety to conceal the dependence of the adored master on his teacher for the fact that until Herculaneum began to yield up its secrets, Nausiphanes was no more than an empty name to us. This vulgar self-exaltation by abuse of the very persons to whom one is indebted for all one's ideas distinguishes Epicurus from all the other Greek thinkers who have made a name for themselves. Plato is almost over-anxious to mark his debt to his Pythagorean teachers,

and the way in which he does so, by putting discoveries of his own into the mouth of the Pythagorean
astronomer Timaeus, has played sad havoc with the
histories of Greek science. Aristotle has undoubtedly
rather more self-importance then is good for most men,
but even he stops short at regarding his own system
as the final philosophy towards which his predecessors
were unconsciously progressing. It was reserved for
Epicurus to put forward a clumsy amalgam of inconsistent beliefs, and to trust to bluster to conceal the
sources of his borrowings.

A few words may be said here as to the amount of
the extant remains of Epicurean literature, and the
later fortune of the School. Of the actual works of
Epicurus the whole has perished, apart from scattered
fragments preserved in quotations of later authors,
mostly unfriendly. We possess, however, two undoubtedly genuine letters, one to Herodotus on the
general principles of Epicurean Atomism, and another
to Menoeceus containing a summary of ethical teaching,
both inserted in Diogenes' *Life*. The *Life* also contains
two other documents, purporting to be by Epicurus,
(1) a letter to Pythocles on astronomy and meteorology,
and (2) a set of κύριαι δόξαι or *Select Apophthegms* forming
a brief catechism of the main points of the doctrine.

The accuracy of the first of these is evinced by its
close agreement with what we are told by later authors
of the physical doctrine of Epicurus, particularly with
the corresponding sections of the poem of Lucretius.

EPICURUS

This letter cannot possibly be a genuine work of Epicurus, and we know from Philodemus that even in his own time (first century B.C.) its authenticity was doubted. It is pretty certainly an excerpt made by some early Epicurean from the voluminous lost work on *Physics* and thrown into epistolary form in imitation of the two genuine letters. As to the second document, it was known to Philodemus and Cicero under its present title, and appears, as Usener holds, to be an early compendium made up of verbal extracts of what were considered the most important statements in the works of Epicurus and his leading friends. There are also a large number of moral apophthegms either quoted as Epicurean or demonstrably of Epicurean authorship embedded in Cicero, Seneca, Plutarch, Porphyry, the Anthology of Stobaeus and elsewhere. Usener has shown that the chief source of these sayings must have been an epitome of the correspondence between Epicurus and his three chief friends, Metrodorus, Polyaenus, and Hermarchus, the four recognised καθηγεμόνες or 'doctors' of the sect. From later Epicureans we have the great poem of Lucretius who can be shown in general to have followed his master very closely, though in what strikes a modern reader as his highest scientific achievement, his anticipations of the doctrine of the evolution of species, he is probably reproducing not Epicurus but his own poetical model Empedocles. The excavation of Herculaneum, and the subsequent deci-

pherment of the papyri found there, has also put us
in possession of a great deal of very second-rate stuff
from the hand of Philodemus.

A word as to the subsequent fate of the School.
The two chief characteristics of the sect, as remarked
by the ancients, were the warmth of the friendship
subsisting between its members, and their absolute
unity of opinion, which last, however, had its bad
side, since, as the ancients complain, the chief reason
of the absence of controversies is that the Epicureans
read nothing but the works of Epicurus and the
καθηγεμόνες, and treat them as infallible scriptures,
even being expected to learn the *Catechism* by
heart. A third peculiarity was the almost idolatrous
adoration paid to the founder who, as we see from
Lucretius, was regarded as all but divine, as the
one and only man who had redeemed the race from
universal misery by pointing out the path to true
happiness.

It has been remarked that the Epicurean society in
many ways is more like the early Christian Church
than it is like a scientific school. Thus (1) it is not
so much a band of thinkers as a group of persons
united by a common rule of life. (We must remember, however, that this 'religious' side to the
association between the members of a 'school' belong
equally to Pythagoreanism and Platonism.) (2) Like
the Christians, the Epicureans are primarily united by
the 'love of the brethren,' and by a common devotion

to a personal founder who is regarded rather as a
Redeemer from misery than as an intellectual teacher
(though here, too, we must not forget that Pythagoras
was equally to his early disciples a divine or semi-
divine Redeemer, with the difference that with them
it was largely by revealing scientific truth that he was
believed to have effected the redemption). (3) Like
the Church, the Epicurean society is indifferent to
differences of nationality, sex, social status. (4) As
Wallace says, the correspondence of Epicurus and his
friends mixes up high speculative theories with homely
matters of every-day life, such as the regulation of
diet, in a way which is equally characteristic of the
New Testament. (5) Epicureanism has also its
analogue to the Christian 'love-feasts' in the monthly
common meals which are provided for by Epicurus in
his will. Similarly his concern for the children of
Metrodorus and for the support of needy and aged
brethren reminds us of the care of the early Christians
for the 'poor saints,' the widows, and the orphans.
The two societies also correspond on their unfavourable
side, in what has always been the great intellectual
sin of the Church, undue readiness to treat its
formulae as infallible and exempt from all examination. The Epicurean who read nothing but the
καθηγεμόνες is the prototype of those modern Christians
who read nothing but the Bible and the approved
commentaries, and regard criticism and free inquiry
as the work of the devil. If the Philosophy of the

Garden had ever become a widely diffused and influential theory of conduct, it must necessarily have plunged the ancient world into the same conflict between 'science' and 'religion' of which we hear too much to-day.

These analogies—though most of them can be to some extent found in other philosophical schools—make it all the more interesting to note that the Epicureans and the Christians, though representing diametrically opposite types of thought, met on common ground as being the only sects who openly repudiated the established religion and scoffed at its apparatus of public ceremonial. The Sceptic avoided the collision easily enough. Precisely because he held that unreasoning faith is involved in all judgments he felt no call to deny the theological belief of his fellows. The Platonist and the Stoic stood to a large extent on common ground with popular religion in their devotion to their belief in Providence and the moral government of the world, to which the Platonist added a fervid faith in Theism and immortality: like Broad Churchmen to-day, they could always acquiesce in the details of popular religion by putting a non-natural interpretation on everything which, in its plain sense, seemed objectionable or absurd. But the Epicurean was cut off from these expedients by the fact that it was one of his cardinal doctrines that 'the gods' exercise no influence on human affairs, as the Christian was by his belief that they were 'idols' or even devils who could not be worshipped without blasphemy against the true God. Not that the Epicureans, like the Christians, refused to take part in the public ceremonial of worship. Philodemus expressly appeals to the exemplary conduct of Epicurus himself on this point. But they made no secret of their scorn for the popular belief in Providence, prayer, and retribution, and hence no amount of external compliance could clear them from the charge of atheism with persons for whom religion was a vital affair.[1] Lucian (second century A.D.) illustrates the point amusingly in his account of the ritual instituted by the charlatan Alexander of Aboni Teichos who set up an oracle which gained great repute and was even once formally consulted by the Emperor Marcus. Among other things, Alexander started a mystical ceremonial from which he used formally to exclude all 'infidels, Christians, and Epicureans.' In the course of the worship he used to cry, 'Away with the Christians!' the congregation giving the response, 'Away with the Epicureans!' the Christians and Epicureans being the two bodies who were persistently infidel from Alexander's point of view. Lucian adds that Alexander solemnly burned the works of the objectionable teacher, and that it was an Epicurean who first exposed the fraudulent

---

[1] As Plutarch says, the Epicurean may go through the ritual of religion, but it can bring him no inward joy, since he regards it as an empty mummery.

trickery of his oracle, and narrowly escaped being lynched by the devout mob for doing so.

Much earlier, probably about 200 B.C., there appear to have been actual persecutions, and perhaps even martyrdoms, of Epicureans in various Greek cities, and we know that works were published in the style of the religious tracts of our own day, relating the judgments of Heaven on Epicureans and their miraculous conversions.

As to the internal history of the sect there is not much to be said, since, as we have seen, they were too indifferent to speculation to make any important innovations on the original teaching of the 'doctors,' though, as we have yet to see, there was at least some attempt to lay the foundations of an Inductive Method in logic. The School continued to flourish as a distinct sect well down into the third century after Christ. The names of a number of prominent Epicureans of the first century B.C. are well known to us from Cicero, who had himself attended the lectures of two of them, Phaedrus and Zeno of Sidon. (It should be mentioned that before Cicero's time the house of Epicurus in Melite had fallen into ruins and the gardens of the philosophical sects had been ruined in the cruel siege of Athens by Sulla.)

When Greek philosophy began to make its appearance in Rome itself the first system to be so transferred was the Epicurean. Cicero mentions as the first Latin writers on Epicureanism Gaius Amafinius

EPICURUS

(*Tusculan Disputations*, iv. 6) and Rabirius (*Academics*, i. 5), and speaks vaguely of their being followed by many others. He finds much fault both with the literary style of these writers and with the want of arrangement in their works, but says that the doctrine made rapid headway owing to its unscientific character and apparent simplicity. It is not clear whether these Latin prose works were earlier or later than the great poem of Lucretius. Lucretius, according to St. Jerome, lived from 94 to 53 B.C., wrote his poem in the intervals of an insanity brought on by a love-potion, and ended by his own hand. The poem was polished up by Cicero. A comparison with Donatus's *Life of Virgil* shows that Jerome's dates are a few years out, and that the real dates for the poet's birth and death should probably be 99/98—55 B.C. The meaning of the remark about Cicero is probably that Cicero edited the poem for circulation after the author's death. Munro has shown that the Cicero meant is pretty certainly the famous Marcus, and the fact of his connection with the work is made all the more likely since the only contemporary allusion to it occurs in a letter from Marcus to his brother Quintus, then serving on Caesar's staff in Britain and Gaul, written early in the year 54 (*Epp. ad Quintum Fratrem*, ii. 11). The 'editing' cannot have been at all carefully done, as the poem is notoriously in a most disjointed state. According to the manuscripts Cicero tells his brother that it is a work exhibiting both genius and art (which is, in fact, the case), but most modern editors make him underrate the poem by inserting a negative with one or other of the two clauses. The influence of Lucretius on the poets of the Augustan age, such as Virgil, Ovid, Manilius, belongs to the history of literature, not to that of philosophy.

To the same general period as Lucretius belongs Philodemus from whom so many fragments have been discovered in the rolls brought from Herculaneum, and who lived under the protection of Cicero's enemy L. Calpurnius Piso, the father-in-law of Caesar. Another well-known Roman Epicurean is Titus Pomponius Atticus, the life-long friend and correspondent of Cicero. Gaius Cassius Longinus, the real author of the conspiracy against Caesar, is also said to have belonged to the sect, to which, it must be owned, he did no credit. Horace's profession of Epicureanism is well known, though we may be sure that his interest in the system was confined to its ethical side. A later and greater writer who, without being a member of any sect, was largely in sympathy with the spirit of the Epicureans and shared their veneration for Epicurus as the deliverer of mankind from degrading superstition, is Lucian of Samosata (second century A.D.). There is some evidence that the popularity of the doctrine was augmented in the second century of our era. Plutarch and Galen, in this century, found it worth while to revive the polemic against Epicurus which had been originated in his own lifetime by

EPICURUS

Plato's Academy, and steadily kept up until it took a Latin dress in the ridicule which Cicero's Academic and Stoic characters are made to pour on the School in his philosophical dialogues. When the Emperor Marcus endowed the chairs of Philosophy at Athens at the expense of the state, Epicureanism, as well as Platonism, Aristotelianism and Stoicism figured among the state-supported doctrines.

Naturally enough, as the Christian Church became more powerful and more dogmatic, it found itself in violent conflict with the anti-theological ideas of Epicurus, and such writers as Lactantius (end of third century A.D.) made him a special object of invective, thereby unconsciously contributing to increase our stock of Epicurean fragments. By the middle of the fourth century the School had fallen into oblivion, and the Emperor Julian (reigned 360-363 A.D.) congratulates himself on the fact that most even of their books are no longer in circulation. Towards the end of the century St. Augustine declares that even in the pagan schools of rhetoric their opinions had become wholly forgotten. (*Epist.*, 118, 21).

CHAPTER II

THE NATURE OF REALITY

1. *The parts of Philosophy.*   It is specially characteristic of Epicurus that his conception of the end to be
aimed at by Philosophy is narrowly and exclusively
practical; in fact, his School might be named not
inaptly the Pragmatists of Antiquity. As Sextus
Empiricus puts it (*adv. Mathematicos*, xi. 169): 'Epicurus
used to say that Philosophy is an activity which by
means of reasoning and discussion produces a happy
life.'   And we have a saying of Epicurus himself that
'we must not make a mere pretence of Philosophy,
but must be real philosophers, just as we need not the
pretence but the reality of health.'   And again, 'The
discourse of philosophers by whom none of our passions
are healed is but idle.   Just as medicine is useless
unless it expels disease from the body, so Philosophy
is useless unless it expels passion from the soul.'   In
this conception of the philosopher as the healer of the
sick soul, and of Philosophy as the medicine he
employs, Epicurus is, of course, saying no new thing.
The thought that the work of Philosophy is to produce
health of soul, and that virtue is to the soul what

35

health is to the body, goes back in the last resort to the Pythagorean medical men of Magna Graecia, and is, for the attentive student, the key to the whole moral doctrine of Plato and Aristotle. Where Epicurus is at variance with Plato and Aristotle is in holding that mental enlightenment, the understanding of things as they truly are, is not itself an integral part of 'salvation,' or the 'soul's health,' but a mere means to it. Hence he sets no store on science except as a means to something beyond itself. He despises history, mathematics, and literary cultivation on the ground that they do not bear upon conduct. In an extant fragment of a letter he says, with a heated outburst of language, 'For God's sake, crowd on sail and flee from all "culture"' (Usener, Fr. 163); and in another, 'I congratulate you on having come to Philosophy undefiled by any "culture"' (Fr. 117). Epicurus is constantly attacked by his later critics for this contempt of polite education, but he may, of course, mean no more than that his mission is not only to the wise and prudent, but to all who fear and suffer. There is to be a place in his scheme for the homely and humble, the babes and sucklings, as well as for the wise in the wisdom of this world.

The only science to which he attaches any value is Physics (φυσιολογία, the general theory of the constitution of the universe), and he values Physics simply for its moral effect. By giving a purely naturalistic theory of the world, Physics frees us from all belief in the agency of God or the gods, and thus delivers us from the dread of God's judgments, and from anxious striving to win His favour. By proving the mortality of the soul it sets us free from superstitious terror about the unknown future. By teaching us to distinguish between what is necessary to support our health and what is superfluous, it teaches us to limit our desires to things convenient for us, and emancipates us from bondage to the lust of the eye and the pride of life. But for these services, Physics would have no worth. As Epicurus himself puts it in § 10 of his *Catechism* : 'If our apprehensions about appearances in the heavens, and about death and its possible consequences, and also our ignorance of the limits of pain and desire, gave us no uneasiness, we should have had no need of a science of nature.' Similarly Lucretius explains that the whole object of his poem is to show that the world has been produced without divine agency (*opera sine divom*), and that there is no pain to be feared after death. Science is, in fact, valuable solely because it banishes God from the world, and proves the mortality of the soul, and so, as Lucretius puts it, 'religion—the vague dread of the unknown—is put under foot and man brought level with heaven.'

Hence, along with all speculative science, Epicurus professed to reject as useless the syllogistic Logic of the Academy and Aristotle. Of the three divisions of Philosophy as fixed by Xenocrates, Logic, Physics, Ethics, the doctrines of discourse, of nature, of conduct,

Epicurus dispenses wholly with the first, and retains the second simply as a necessary introduction to the third.

Still, of course, though agreeing with our modern empiricists in the rejection of formal deductive Logic, he requires some doctrine of method, some theory of the way in which true generalisations may be obtained, and some standard of truth and falsehood. To meet this need, Epicurus and his followers tried to lay down rules of what we should call inductive Logic, rules showing how a true inference may be drawn from the data of sense-perception. This rudimentary theory of induction they called *Canonics*, the doctrine of the κανὼν or *rule* by which inferences may be drawn from particular observations. Hence, finally, the school divided Philosophy into three parts, Canonics, Physics, Ethics, of which the two former are only valuable because they are requisite for the last. This is what Seneca means when he says (*Ep.*, 89. 11), 'the Epicureans hold that there are two parts of Philosophy, the Natural and the Moral, but reject the Rational part [*i.e.* Formal Logic, the doctrine of syllogism]. But since they were forced by the nature of things to remove ambiguities, and to detect falsities concealed under an appearance of truth, they too introduce a branch of study which they call the doctrine of judgment, and its standard (*de iudicio et regula* = περὶ τοῦ κανόνος), which is the rational part of Philosophy under another name. But they regard this as a mere complement of Natural Philosophy.'

THE NATURE OF REALITY

2. *Canonics—the Rules of Philosophising.* The Epicurean doctrine of the κανὼν or rule of generalisation is
so crude that one would not naturally expect it to
exhibit signs of having been borrowed from a foreign
source. Yet here, as everywhere in Epicurus, we
come on signs of indebtedness to others for the views
on which he plumed himself. We have already
read in the *Life* by Diogenes that Antigonus of
Carystus regarded the whole doctrine of the Canon
as a plagiarism from Nausiphanes. Now the fact that
before Epicurus set up for himself as an independent
philosopher he had been a pupil of Nausiphanes may
be regarded as certain, since the statement comes to us
on the double authority of Antigonus and Apollodorus,
the latter of whom may fairly be taken as representing
Eratosthenes. From the frequent recurrence of it in
writers like Cicero and Plutarch we may infer that
the later Epicureans were unable to deny it, and the
extreme scurrility with which Epicurus himself spoke
of Nausiphanes as a person who claimed to have
taught him his Philosophy is enough to show that he
had at some time stood in a relation of dependence on
the former which he wished afterwards to disguise.
We have further the warrant of two of Epicurus' chief
friends, Leonteus and Metrodorus, for the positive
statement that Epicurus originally called himself a
Democritean (Plutarch *Against Colotes*, 3), though he
afterwards reviled Democritus with his usual coarse-
ness. When we come to deal with the Epicurean

doctrine of atoms we shall see that these statements must in the main be true; Epicurean Atomism is unintelligible except as a clumsy attempt on the part of an incoherent thinker to adapt the general physical doctrine of Democritus to views which had been made current in Athens by Aristotle, which are really incompatible with it. Nausiphanes, of whom we know that he combined the physics of Democritus with the ethical agnosticism of Pyrrho, thus appears as the indispensable link of connection between Epicurus and the early science of Ionia, and we may see reason to think that there may be a great deal of truth in a statement made by Sextus Empiricus about the origin of Epicurus' blind hatred of mathematics. It was due, Sextus says, to his 'animosity against Nausiphanes, the disciple of Pyrrho, who had a large following of younger men, and made serious studies of mathematics, and even more specially of rhetoric. Epicurus had been his pupil, but from a desire to be thought a self-taught philosopher of original genius did his best to deny the fact. He was anxious to obliterate the reputation of Nausiphanes, and so volubly denounces the mathematical studies in which the latter enjoyed great renown' (*adv. Mathematicos*, i. 2). Sextus then goes on to quote the abusive letter to 'the philosophers of Mytilene,' in which Epicurus nicknames Nausiphanes 'the Mollusc,' and winds up by saying that 'he was a worthless fellow and devoted to pursuits from which one cannot possibly arrive at wisdom': by which, says

Sextus, he means mathematics. Some information about the contents of the work called the *Tripod* has been preserved in Philodemus *On Rhetoric*. Most of what Philodemus has to say is very vague, but we can make out quite clearly that Nausiphanes was anxious to show that the combination of an eloquent and attractive style with mathematical and physical research is both feasible and desirable. He aims, in fact, at such a combination of these qualities as we see in a man like W. K. Clifford, who united high mathematical gifts with the ability to make the general results of abstruse research intelligible and attractive to the ordinary man of average education. It is strongly corroborative of the assertions of Antigonus and Apollodorus that we find Nausiphanes employing the very term which was afterwards used by Epicurus as the technical word for 'inductive generalisation' (ἐπιλογιστικὴ θεωρία=induction from the known facts of sense, the Epicurean ἐπιλογισμός).[1] It has even been suggested that Nausiphanes had anticipated Aristotle in appropriating the word 'syllogism,' the casting up of an account, computation of a sum total, in the

---

[1] See the full text of the relevant passages of Philodemus in Diels, *Fragmente der Vorsokratiker*, 1. 464-465. As to dates, Nausiphanes is regularly said to have 'heard' Democritus in person. If this is true he must have been at least some years older than Aristotle (born 384 B.C.), since Democritus was certainly born about 460, and even if he lived, as tradition asserts, to over a hundred, he can hardly have been actively teaching in the last decade of his life

technical logical sense, but in the absence of precise dates it would be rash to be dogmatic on the point. It is equally possible that the word came to both Aristotle and Nausiphanes from the Platonic Academy. For the present we had better confine ourselves to the statement that the Epicurean theory of knowledge probably comes from the same source as the Epicurean borrowings from the Physics and Ethics of Democritus, viz., Nausiphanes. We shall see, as we go on, that the theory is not that of Democritus, and is really inconsistent with physical Atomism.

Epicurus starts then, just like a modern empiricist, with the unproved assertion that all our knowledge and all our concepts are derived solely from sensation. 'Whatever we cognize,' so Cicero expresses the doctrine in *De Finibus*, i. 64, 'has its origin in the senses.' Epicurus himself says in § 23 of the *Catechism*, that unqualified scepticism about the veracity of sensation is self-destructive. 'If you attack all sensations you will have no standard left by which to condemn those of them which you pronounce false.' Thus, be it noted, he supposes it conceded that some sensations at least are veridical, the very point which the theory of Democritus had quite consistently denied. Since the atomic theory, which Democritus regards as absolutely true, is obviously at variance with the testimony of the senses, Democritus had drawn the conclusion that it is only reflection or reasoning, never sensation, which apprehends reality. No thing really has the character which it seems to our senses to have, and the fundamental proposition of a true theory of knowledge is that sensation is inherently misleading. 'There are two types of cognition, the one genuine, the other bastard. To the bastard kind belong all such things as sight, hearing, smell, taste, touch; but the genuine is separate from it' (Sextus Empiricus, *adv. Math.*, vii. 135, who explains rightly that the contrast is between sensation and 'understanding').[1] Some such view is, of course, indispensable to any Philosophy which holds that the physical world consists simply of atoms in motion, and the rejection of it by Epicurus is only a sign of his entire lack of intellectual thoroughness.

All knowledge then begins with, and can be analysed back into, actual sensations. And Epicurus is as confident as Locke that sensation always has a real external object, and is not a mere subjective affection of our mind or our nervous system. Unlike Locke, he goes so far as to hold that sensation not only has such an object, but that it always represents its object exactly as it really is: 'it is a property of sensation

[1] Democritus, Fr. 11 (Diels). The names for the two kinds of cognition are γνησίη (legitimate), σκοτίη (lit. 'dark'). I assume that σκοτίη here is used metaphorically in the sense of 'bastard,' 'begotten under the cover of secrecy,' as in the common tragic periphrases σκότιον λέχος, κρύφιον λέχος for 'concubine.' So Diels renders the word by *unecht*, 'spurious.' I find that the right rendering has also already been given by Professor Burnet and others.

alone to apprehend the present object which arouses it' (Fr. 247). Or more precisely, to quote Sextus again, 'Sensation, because it apprehends the objects which fall under it without subtraction, addition, or transposition, since it is irrational, is always completely true, and apprehends existence as it veritably is' ✓ (*op. cit.* viii. 9). Sensations were therefore called ἐνάργειαι, 'clear and evident' cognitions, and it was maintained that even the sensations of dreamers and lunatics are strictly veridical, because they are 'changes in consciousness,' and a change must always have a real cause (Fr. 63). We see, then, that Epicurus, like Locke, holds that there is an indefinable something about every actual sensation which distinguishes it from any other mode of being conscious, such as memory or imagination; you cannot say what this difference consists in, but you directly feel it; every sensation carries with it the stamp of its own 'reality.' It is interesting to observe the reason given for the view that sensation always has an external object. The argument is that the sensation is always *caused* by some thing. Leaving on one side the question of fact raised by some modern psychologists as to the existence of 'centrally initiated sensations,' we see at once that Epicurus is thus attempting to guarantee the objectivity of sense-qualities by appealing to a *universal law* of causation. This is quite inconsistent with his empiricist starting-point, but the inconsistency is one in which he has inevitably been followed by all later empiricists. We see also that he falls into the very common error of confusing the objects perceived by the senses with the physical stimuli which arouse sensation, (like modern writers who talk of the eye as perceiving light-waves, forgetting that what we perceive is not vibrations but colours).

To the question why he holds that sensation not only has an external existing cause, but always perceives that cause just as it is, Epicurus replies that a sensation is ἄλογόν τι, non-rational, and therefore neither adds to, takes away from, nor transposes the parts of its object, since all these are operations of the reflective understanding. Hence the very non-rational character of sensation becomes a guarantee of its fidelity as a record of external fact. Hence Epicurus, thanks to his indifference to the theory of knowledge, cannot like Locke distinguish between the primary sensations and the secondary, and does not even appear to see that there is any problem involved, though one would have thought that his adherence to Atomism must have forced the question on his notice.

For the full explanation of the theory that sensation is always unerring we need for a moment to anticipate our account of the Epicurean Physics. The explanation turns on a distinction between the immediate and the mediate object in sense-perception. When a distant tower which is really square appears round, have we not an illusion of sight? Epicurus says no; there is only a fallacy of inference. The square tower throws off a series of images, or atomic skins from its surface. These images are originally square also, but being material, like the tower itself, they clash with other bodies as they travel from the tower towards the eye, and thus get their angles rounded off. What we actually perceive, the inner or immediate object as we might call it, is one of these 'skins,' and this has become round before it strikes on the sensory organ, and is therefore perceived exactly as it is. The error lies simply in the judgment that the mediate object, the body from which the 'skin' was thrown off, is round too, and so the fallacy belongs entirely to reason and not to sense. This explains also what was meant by saying that the sensations of a dreamer or a lunatic are veridical. Like all sensations, they have a cause external to the percipient, and this cause is, as always, a 'skin' composed of atoms. The dreamer or lunatic apprehends this 'skin' just as it is when it acts on his sensory system, and his sensation is therefore 'true'; his error lies in the inference he makes as to the body from which the 'skin' has been projected. For example, some of the 'skins' may never have been thrown off from any single actual body at all. They may be accidental agglomerations of atoms originally coming from different sources, formed in the process of transit through the intervening space, *e.g.* the images of a three-headed giant or of a centaur. If the madman takes these for 'skins' thrown off from real bodies of giants or centaurs, he commits a fallacy of inference. Hence it is essential to the theory to distinguish very sharply between actual sensation and its reproduction in memory or imagination, which may be distorted by such fallacies to any extent. (See Epicurus' own words in Fr. 36.) Unfortunately Epicurus gives us no rule by which to make the distinction.

The next step taken by Epicurus is to explain the nature of what he calls a πρόληψις, or *pre-notion*. By this he means the general notion or concept of a class of things. He takes it, precisely in the fashion of Huxley, to be the same thing as a mental 'composite photograph,' resulting from the blending into one memory-image of a number of residues of individual sensations. 'All our concepts,' he says (Fr. 36), 'have been derived from sensations by contiguity, analogy, similarity, and composition, reasoning also contributing to the result.' His view then, like that of our Associationists, is clearly that perception of concrete things begins with an association in thought of sense-qualities which have been presented together. Further association by similarity, whether of relations or of qualities, as well as conscious combination in accord with what we should call some category or principle of order, supervenes, and so, in the end, out of a number of individual sensations, occurring at different times and having individual qualitative differences, is formed a general or typical image, not corresponding exactly to any one presented object, but representing the features in which the members of a kindred group of objects are alike. (I seem to trace in this account a psychologically crude reproduction of Aristotle's account of the way in which 'many memories of the same thing' give rise to a single experience.) This 'generic image' is what Epicurus calls a πρόληψις or pre-notion and defines as 'a true conception, or belief, or general notion stored up in the mind, that is, the recollection of what has frequently been presented from without; for as soon as the word "man" is uttered, we think by a "pre-notion" of the generic type of "man," our sensations being the origin from which this is derived' (Diogenes, x. 33). Now Epicurus demands of a correctly-formed 'pre-notion,' just as he did of sensation, that it shall be ἐναργές, 'clear and distinct'; and by this he means not that it shall be logically *well-defined*, but that we shall have a clear-cut picture of it before the imagination. Hence, like Berkeley, he holds that if words are to have a meaning, the simple and primary senses of them must represent perfectly definite mental pictures. The primary meaning of a name is always 'clear and distinct'; we never could apply a significant name to anything, if we had not first become acquainted with the type or class to which the thing belongs by a 'pre-notion.' Hence 'pre-notions' are all 'clear and distinct.' Clearly we have here a theory of the formation of concepts which is virtually that commonly ascribed to Locke, except that Epicurus actually believes the processes of association and combination of which he speaks to be quite literally actions of a *material* thing (a complex of atoms which has made its way into the organism through the sense-organs), on a second material thing, —the so-called soul. We have also the same confusion which besets the modern psychologising empiricists between a logically universal concept and a mental 'composite photograph' which leads to the error of supposing that what cannot be pictured cannot be well defined. In fact it is often just the things which are hardest to picture which can be most readily defined for the understanding. Thus in arithmetic a 'rational number,' in geometry a curve which passes through all the points of a given area, are notions which are clear and distinct for the understanding, since we know exactly what we mean by them, but they can be imagined, if at all, only in the vaguest way. Or again, I may know perfectly well what the law means by 'wilful murder,' but the mental picture which I form on hearing the words may be absurdly sketchy and indistinct, or I may even form no picture at all.

We see now what the Epicurean standard of 'reality' or 'truth' will be in the case of the sensation and the general notion. The individual sensation carries an assurance of objective reality with it in an indescribable way; we *feel* that it is real, just as Locke says that we have an immediate feeling of the difference between actually being in the fire and merely imagining ourselves there. And Epicurus

goes on to argue that if you have apparently conflicting sensations, you must not deny the reality of either.
One sensation cannot prove the falsity of another of
the same kind, for both have exactly the same evidence
for them, nor can the truthfulness of a sensation be
disproved by an appeal to those of a different sense,
since the objects apprehended by the different senses
are disparate. (This seems meant to exclude, *e.g.*
the correction of a visual judgment of form by appeal
to experiences of touch. Presumably both experiences
are regarded as equally 'real,' but as concerned with
different immediate objects.) Nor can you be argued
out of your sensations by reasoning, since all reasoning
is founded on sensation (Fr. 36).

So in the case of the 'pre-notion,' its objectivity,
like that of the sensations from which it is com-
pounded, is supposed to be shown by its possessing,
like them, an irresistible 'clearness and distinctness';
it is clear-cut and definite and, as Hume would say,
strikes the mind with a peculiar force and liveliness,
and it is this liveliness which guarantees that it is
objectively 'true'—*i.e.* based on genuine sensation.
Similarly with feeling in the modern sense; pleasures
are held to carry in themselves the stamp of their own
reality (see Fr. 260). Hence the summary statement
of the doxographers that 'according to Epicurus the
"criteria" are sensations, pre-notions, and feelings'
(πάθη).

But now, to come to what is the fundamental point

in the whole theory, what is the standard of 'reality'
or 'truth' in *opinions*, *i.e.* in beliefs or judgments?
(It is really only in relation to beliefs that we can
rationally ask for such a standard; there is no sense
in calling a sensation or a generic image, as distinct
from a belief about it, true or false at all.) It cannot, of
course, be maintained that *all* beliefs are true. Some
of them are certainly false; but is there any means of
knowing the false beliefs from the true? Epicurus says
'if a belief is witnessed to, or at least not witnessed
against by our clear and evident perceptions, it is true;
if it is witnessed against, or not witnessed to, it is false'
(Fr. 247). Or, in other words, a belief is true when it
is confirmed by the evidence of the senses, false when
it is contradicted by that evidence; where there is
neither confirmation nor contradiction, the belief may
be true or may be false. This is, to be sure, the view
regularly taken by pure empiricists as to the conditions
under which a scientific hypothesis may be regarded
as established. It is established when its consequences
are found to be verified by sense-experience, confuted
when they are found to be in conflict with sense-
experience. The point is of special moment for
Epicurus because, with all the sensationalism of his
theory of cognition, his Physics are entirely built on
a doctrine about certain things (the atoms and the
empty space in which they move), which admittedly
cannot be perceived at all. How then can we have
any test of its truth? The Epicurean answer to

51

this question is quite different from that given by Democritus. Democritus, as we saw, regarded sense-perception as inherently illusory; consequently he makes no attempt whatever to appeal to the senses in support of the atomic theory. With him, as with his predecessor Leucippus, the doctrine is put forward as a metaphysical deduction from the two premisses (1) What *is* is immutable; (2) motion is a fact. The immediate conclusion from these premisses is that what *is* consists of absolutely unchanging units moving about, approaching, and receding, in empty space. Epicurus is bound, on the other hand, to achieve the impossible task of showing that Atomism is compatible with the view that our sensations are the criteria of reality. 'We must draw our inferences,' he says,' 'from the perceptible to the imperceptible' (Fr. 36). What he urges is, in effect, that the doctrine of atoms is established *if* it leads to a conception of the world conformable to our sense-experience, and if the properties and motions we suppose in the atoms are analogous with our sense-experience of those of perceptible things. But here a difficulty at once arises. The atomic hypothesis of the world's structure might not be the only one which would yield results consonant with sense-experience; a plurality of different theories might all be 'witnessed to, or not witnessed against, by our senses.' Why then should we give any one of them a preference over any other? It is clearly with a view to this difficulty that Epicurus puts forward a theory in which he anticipates both Hobbes and—may we not say?—our modern Pragmatists. Two inconsistent explanations of the same fact may be equally true and equally valuable, if either would yield results conformable with sense-experience. Now the sole utility of the study of Physics was to lie in its power to produce serenity of mind by expelling the fear of a judgment after death and the belief in Divine control of the course of events. Hence if there are several theories about the cause of a natural event which all agree in being purely naturalistic, and if the result would equally occur on any one of these suppositions, Epicurus teaches that any one of them is as good as any other, and we have no reason to decide between them, since the practical consequences for life are the same. Thus, while certain theories are laid down as absolutely true, *e.g.* the doctrine of Atoms (on the ground that they are requisite for *any* purely mechanical theory of nature), alternative causes are assigned for most of the special phenomena. This comes out repeatedly in the epitome of the work on *Physics* which forms the so-called second 'letter' given by Diogenes. We are there told that appearances in the heavens are capable of a plurality of different explanations all equally accordant with sense-perception, and we must not prefer one of these to another. 'For Philosophy should not proceed in accord with empty dogmas and postulates but only as actual appearances demand. For what life requires is

not unreason and idle opinion, but a tranquil existence' ([*Ep.*] ii. 3; Usener, p. 36). Thus Epicurus not
merely says what is true enough, that in our present
state of knowledge ascertained facts may often be
accounted for on rival hypotheses; he actually forbids
the extension of science by the devising of experiments
to reduce the number of possible explanations. Any
explanation will do, if it only excludes Divine agency.
We may fairly say, then, that what recommends the
atomic theory to Epicurus is not its scientific advan-
tages, but its utility as a means of getting rid of
Theism. And we must further note that his reason
for wishing to banish theistic hypotheses from science
is not the legitimate one that as descriptions of *how*
events succeed one another they leave us just where
they found us, but the illegitimate one that he
personally dislikes the thought of a God whose
judgments may possibly have to be reckoned with
hereafter.

Whether Epicurus devised for himself the singular
combination of two such incompatibles as Democritean
Atomism and absolute sensationalism or borrowed it
from Nausiphanes there appears to be nothing to show,
unless we may regard the evidence of Philodemus,
which proves that Nausiphanes had been interested in
the inductive problem of inferring the unperceived
from the perceived, as an indication of borrowing.
Such a problem could hardly have appealed to a
disciple of Democritus unless he had entered on the

path of trying to combine his master's Physics with sensationalism. Hence it may well be that Epicurus is as unoriginal here as he shows himself everywhere else.

We may also note that the Epicurean doctrine of the criterion, taken as it stands, is quite inconsistent with the rejection of Formal Logic. Before we can say whether the results which 'follow from' an hypothesis are 'confirmed by sense-experience,' we must know what results *do* follow and what do not, and how are we to know this without any doctrine of deductive Logic? How can we tell whether we are reasoning rightly or wrongly from the perceptible to the imperceptible without some doctrine of the conditions under which generalisation is sound? Later Epicureans appear to have tried to fill the gap left at this point by Epicurus. Among the remains of Philodemus we find in particular some notes of the teaching of Zeno of Sidon (flor. *c.* 80 B.C.) on this very matter. Zeno admits that a few unusual instances of a sequence are insufficient to establish a general rule, while a complete examination of *all* relevant cases is usually impossible. So he holds that in order to make a safe generalisation we require to examine a number of instances which, though alike in some one respect, vary among themselves in other respects. By comparison we may then discover what has been the one regular concomitant in all these cases of the result we are interested in, and then reason by analogy to the presence of this concomitant in other cases. This is, of course, the same method afterwards called by J. S. Mill the Method of Agreement, and, like that method, is too vague to be of any great value except as a basis for mere suggestions of possible connections in Nature. As Wallace says, Zeno (and we may say the same of Mill) evades the difficulty of saying *how much* resemblance warrants us in regarding a number of facts as forming one 'kind' or 'class' of cases. We may add, I think, a further criticism against the whole conception of 'analogy' from the perceptible as the only method of discovering the 'latent processes' in Nature. Why need the behaviour of ultimate molecular or atomic bodies (if there are such things) be analogous at all with the facts of sense-perception? In fact most theories of Physics ascribe to the simple ultimate elements motions which seem strikingly *unlike* those which fall under direct sense-perception. *E.g.* Newton's first law of Motion or the law of the Conservation of Energy seems at first sight to be *contradicted* by sense-perception. We accept them, not because the processes they assume are *like* what we actually see, but because we can *deduce* the results we see from them.

3. *Physics*—The Structure of the Universe.

From Plutarch (*adv. Colotem*, 3) we learn that Epicurus had at one time, like his teacher Nausiphanes, been content to call himself a Democritean, and when we examine his physical theory we shall find that it is, in fact, merely that of Democritus altered for the worse and cut away from the anti-sensational theory of knowledge with which Democritus had rightly connected it. As Cicero says (*De Finibus*, i. 17), 'In his Physics, of which he makes a special boast, Epicurus is absolutely dependent on others. He repeats the views of Democritus with a few minor changes, and, in my judgment, his pretended improvements are really changes for the worse.' Epicurus then, like the fifth-century philosophers to whom he goes back for his view of the world, is in principle a pure materialist. His two fundamental doctrines, like those of Leucippus and Democritus, are (1) nothing is created out of nothing or annihilated into nothing, (2) nothing exists except bodies and empty space. 'The whole universe is bodies and space, for sensation itself universally testifies that there are bodies, and reason must infer to the imperceptible on the analogy of sensation. And if there were not place, or void, or room, or the intangible as we may also call it, bodies would have nowhere to exist nor wherein to move' (*Ep.* i., Usener, p. 5).

From this he infers that the ultimate bodies are atomic, or indivisible (*i.e.* physically indiscerptible, *not* geometrically unextended), by the argument, that if bodies were infinitely divisible, all bodies could be ultimately broken up into infinitely small parts and thus annihilated. 'We may not believe that a finite body contains an infinite or an indefinitely great number of particles; so we must deny the possibility of infinite subdivision . . . lest we should be forced to admit that what is can be annihilated by the constant pressure of surrounding bodies' (*Ep.* i., Usener, p. 5). Atoms, again, must be incapable of *change*, since, if there is to be no annihilation of what is, there must be a permanent substratum which persists under all change. Hence, while we may attribute to atoms, as to sensible bodies, bulk and shape and weight, we must not ascribe to them any further sensible qualities.

Here we are led into a difficulty due to the inconsistency between Atomism and the sensationalistic theory of knowledge. Democritus had drawn from the variability of the colours, tastes, etc., of the bodies we perceive the conclusion of Locke and Descartes, that such sense-qualities are mere subjective effects of the mechanical properties of bodies on *our* organism. Hence he had held that judgments about the sensible qualities of bodies have no objective validity ; they belong to the 'bastard' form of conviction. 'Things are only sweet or bitter, etc., by convention ; in reality there are only atoms and the void.' Epicurus could not follow him here, since to do so would be fatal to the fundamental doctrine of his *Canonic*, that sensation always represents its immediate external object just as it is, without addition, subtraction or modification. He seems to have tried to reconcile the two views in this way. In every composite body there are atoms of very different sizes and shapes, and consequently these varieties are reproduced in the 'skins' (εἴδωλα) thrown from bodies, which are the immediate stimuli and objects of sensation. But owing to the differences in the constitution of organisms, only some of these may be able to act on a given sense-organ. Hence a thing may appear to different persons to be of different colours, red to you, gray to me (if I am colour-blind). The 'image' or 'skin' itself contains both atoms suited to evoke the sensation 'red' and other fitted to evoke 'gray'; but the one set make their way into your sense-organs the other into mine. The thing actually is at once red (and thus your sensation is 'true,') and gray, (and so mine is true also). Colour, therefore, is not a subjective illusion, but a 'variable quality' (σύμπτωμα, the word seems to be medical, and to mean a 'fit,' or sudden seizure,) of the external body, as distinguished from its συμβεβηκότα, viz.: the *permanent* predicates, which do not thus vary, but, as their name implies, always 'go with' the thing, its *primary* qualities. Cf. *Ep.* i. (Usener, p. 11): 'We must hold that we see and recognise the shapes of things in virtue of the entrance of something from actual bodies. For bodies outside us could not have set the stamp of their colour and shape upon us by means of the air between us and them, or of effluences of any kind proceeding from ourselves to them [this is directed against Aristotle and Plato], so well as on the hypothesis that certain imprints enter into us from external things, preserving their colour and shape, and making their way in accord with the appropriate magnitude into the eye or the mind'; and *ib.* (Usener, p. 22): 'Further, the shapes, colours, magnitudes, and all that is predicated of bodies as an attribute of all bodies, or of all visible bodies, and as knowable by bodily perception, must neither be held to be realities *per se* (which is inconceivable), nor to be simply non-existent, nor to be incorporeal predicates of body, nor parts of it . . .' Immediately on this follows the definition of the συμπτώματα, or variable accidents as distinct from the permanent properties of bodies.

Of course we may retort that this is no solution of the difficulty. A mechanical configuration which awakens the perception of red is not the same as a red thing, and moreover, on Epicurus' own showing, if a thing is both red and gray, and I only perceive it as red, I am not apprehending it 'without subtraction.'[1]

I do not know how to account for the inconsequence of Epicurus in thus making the doctrine of Democritus absurd by combining it with sensationalism, except perhaps on the ground that his theory aims at incorporating the view of Nature which had been just made popular by Aristotle. According to Aristotle, who reverted in this respect to the standpoint of pre-Democritean natural science, the fundamental distinctions in Nature are not geometrical or mechanical, but qualitative, the distinctions between hot, cold; dry, moist; white, black, and the other contrary opposites of sense-perception. The attempt to fuse this point

[1] The indications afforded by Lucretius. ii. 795-816, point to the interpretation I have given in the text.

of view with the rigidly mechanical theory of Atomism was bound to produce strange results, and we shall see that it is probably responsible for another grave departure from Democritus.

Epicurus next infers, like Democritus, that the number of atoms is infinite. The All must be infinite, because whatever is finite has limits, and so has something outside itself, but there can be nothing outside the All. The argument, like most of those we have hitherto seen produced by him, is an old one, as it goes back to the famous Eleatic, Melissus of Samos. It seems to be, when applied to prove the conclusion Epicurus draws from it, a sophism, since it does not follow that because the All has nothing outside it, the *number* of things it contains must be infinite. (Melissus, in fact, used the argument to prove that the All must be *one* just because it is infinite.) But Epicurus adds a further physical reason. 'The All must be infinite both in respect of the number of bodies,(*i.e.* atoms), and in respect of the extent of void. For if the void were infinite, but the number of bodies finite, the bodies would never have remained anywhere, but would have been scattered and dissipated through the void, having nothing to support them and fix them in position when they rebound from collision, and if the void were finite it would not contain the infinity of bodies' (*Ep.* i., Usener, p. 7). I do not see that the argument, which has all the appearance of coming from the fifth century Atomists, is conclusive. It is true that you cannot find room for an infinity of atoms in a limited space, but the proof that the number of, atoms must be infinite if space is unlimited seems unsatisfactory. Even on the supposition of an infinite space with a finite number of atoms in it, why might not the attractive forces, however you conceive them, hold the atoms together indefinitely? Or even if you grant the consequence proved, why should it be absurd to hold that it really will be the fate of the universe to be disintegrated into individual atoms each at an infinite distance from every other? To make it absurd, you would need to prove that the world has already existed for an infinite time, so that the disruption, if it were possible, ought to have occurred already. But Epicurus merely assumes the eternity of the world without proof.

When we come to the theory of the motion of the atom we get at once a fundamental divergence from Democritus which, as the Academic critics observed, shows the inferiority of Epicurus as a scientific thinker. To judge from the criticism of Aristotle, who complains that Democritus had never explained what is the *natural* movement of atoms (*i.e.* how an atom would move if it were not deflected by collision with other atoms), we should suppose that Democritus started with an infinite number of atoms moving in every direction, and we know for certain that he held that atoms move with different velocities, the bulkier more rapidly than the less bulky In this way, when they

come to collide the less bulky atoms are squeezed out-
wards, and form a kind of film round a denser centre.
Whether Democritus believed in absolute direction
in space we are not told, but we have, I think, the
right to infer from the data before us that he made no
use of the antithesis of up and down in his theory, and
did not regard his atoms as 'falling.' In other words,
the ancient tradition, for which we have the express
testimony of Theophrastus, is absolutely correct in
asserting that Democritus did not regard *weight* as
an inherent property of the atom. According to him
the inherent properties of the atom are two, shape and
bulk. Weight was added as a third by Epicurus. In
this Democritus was, of course, right, since the weight
of a body is purely relative to its surroundings, while
its mass (which *is* invariable) would, in the case of an
atom, be strictly proportional to its bulk.

Now Epicurus makes both the assumption (1) that
all atoms have weight, but irrespective of their weight,
move with the same velocity through the void, because
it offers no resistance to them; (2) and that they all
move, until deflected by collision in one and the same
direction, viz. *down*, the reason why they move downwards, rather than in any other direction, being their
weight. Thus we have to think of all atoms as
primarily falling in parallel straight lines, with equal
velocities, towards a fixed plane at an infinite distance,
in the direction from our heads to our feet. Apparently
the assumption of the uniform direction rests on a bad

generalisation from our experience of the falling of
bodies to the earth. The blunder made in this assumption is not, as is often said, that Epicurus believes
in an absolute and not merely a relative difference of
directions in space, but that he treats *gravity* as an
inherent tendency in material particles to move towards a fixed plane in empty space, whereas it is really
a tendency to move in the direction of other material
particles. What he does not see is that a single particle, alone in infinite space, would not gravitate at all,
and that the direction of gravity at different places is
not the same. As to the point about equal velocity,
Democritus was clearly thinking in the right scientific
spirit when he began with the assumption of atoms
moving with every degree of velocity, since no valid
reason can be given for supposing uniformity. Epicurus'
apparent ground for asserting the uniformity, viz.,
that there can be no friction between empty space and
the atoms, is obviously worthless, since it proves no
more than that the velocity of an atom falling through
empty space would, in the absence of all other bodies,
be constant; not that for two atoms, let us say at an
immense distance from each other, it must be the same.
But it is noticeable that he has accidentally stumbled
on a truth about *gravity* which is *not* suggested by our
sensible experience. It is true that in a perfect vacuum
particles would fall towards the centre of a large at-
tracting mass from equal distances in equal time. But
this does not show that all atoms originally move with

equal velocity ; it only shows that that part of the velocity of two bodies which is due to gravitation towards the same fixed third body would be equal in empty space. Of course, neither Democritus nor Epicurus could have worked out a really satisfactory cosmical mechanics, as neither possessed the conceptions of mass and momentum.

We may perhaps conjecture the reason for Epicurus' unscientific depravation of the atomic doctrine as to the movement of the atom. The doctrine that 'up' and 'down' correspond to the distinction between movement from the centre of the universe towards its circumference, and that from its circumference to its centre, is a prominent feature in the philosophy of Aristotle, who combines it with the view that 'heavy bodies' naturally move 'down,' towards the centre, 'light bodies' 'up,' perpendicularly away from the centre. As Professor Burnet says, this doctrine led to no serious difficulties in the Aristotelian Physics, because Aristotle thought that there is only one world, and does not attribute weight to the 'heavens' which bound it. The real confusions only come out when the theory of the tendency of heavy bodies to fall 'down' towards a fixed centre is combined with the belief in an infinite void. This unhappy combination of incompatibles looks, as Burnet says, as though it were definitely intended to meet Aristotle's unwise criticism of Democritus and Leucippus by ascribing one and the same 'natural' movement to all atoms. In that case we must ascribe the doctrine to Epicurus, *not to any prede-cessor*, and it will be clear that the only original feature of his system is just the most illogical thing in it.[1]

We come now to the crowning absurdity of the whole scheme. If the atoms all fall perpendicularly, from all eternity, in the same direction and with uniform velocity, obviously no atom should overtake another, and no compound bodies should ever be formed. Instead of a world or worlds of such bodies there ought to be at every moment a downward rain of atoms preserving their original distances from each other, and the condition of the universe at any moment ought to be indistinguishable from its condition at any other. This is obviously not the case, though it is exactly what would happen if the *whole* motion of each particle were due solely, as we should say, to gravitation. To reconcile his first hypothesis about the motion of the atom with sensible fact, Epicurus has to make a second assumption which virtually ruins his fundamental theory that the course of Nature is mechanical. He assumed that at certain moments which we cannot predict, and for no assignable cause, the atom may swerve to a very slight degree out of the path of perpendicular descent. These incalculable swervings, often enough repeated, may lead to a notable deflec-

[1] See Burnet, *Early Greek Philosophy*, 396-397. I have tried to show that his theory of Epicureanism as a conflation of Democritus with Aristotle is confirmed by other inconsistencies in Epicurus which are most naturally explained in the same way.

tion of the atom's path. In this way atoms may come to collide and adhere, and so, in process of time, to form a world of perceptible compound bodies. This is the doctrine of the declination (παρέγκλισις, *clinamen*) of the atom expounded by Lucretius in Book ii. 217 ff. No confirmation of the theory is offered except that given by Lucretius, the existence of unmotived free-will in animals. On the theory that the soul, like everything except the void, is made of atoms, Lucretius argues, you cannot account for volition, or escape fatalism, except by endowing the atoms with the capacity for capricious deviation from their regular paths. Now the Epicu-reans were determined to uphold free-will in the sense of absolutely unmotived volition against the Stoic determinism. Epicurus himself had said (*Ep.* iii., Usener, p. 15), 'It would be better to believe the tale about the gods than to be enslaved to the Destiny of the physicists ; the former leaves a prospect of changing the purposes of the gods by propitiating them, the latter sets up a necessity which cannot be propitiated.' Thus the source of the doctrine was simply a desire to avoid a practically uncomfortable conclusion. Instead of trying to show that rigid determinism is false, Epicurus merely declines to believe in it, though it is a logical consequence of the mechanical view of things, because he dislikes the influence of the belief on human happiness. He then uses this appeal to prejudice, to bolster up his absurd natural science. (That the free-will of Epicurus really means pure caprice, not, as has been sometimes fancied, rational self-determination, is shown *e.g.* by Lucretius ii. 299, where the poet adds to his previous mistaken assertion that weight *is* an internal cause of movement the remark that the 'declination' of the atom at uncertain times and places shows that there is no internal necessity in the behaviour of the mind. Carneades, the great sceptic, correctly remarked (Cicero, *de Fato*, 23) that Epicurus might have defended freedom without the extravagant fiction of παρέγκλισις, if he had simply said that the cause of a voluntary action is not external to the mind. This, however, would have been fatal to his materialistic theory of the mind as a complex of atoms.)

The unscientific character of this method of saving one unprovable hypothesis by a second which really contradicts the first formed one of the standing grounds for censure of Epicurus in antiquity. Cicero sums up the Academic criticism when he says, 'He holds that solid atoms fall downward by their own weight in straight lines, and that this is the natural movement of all bodies. Then it occurred to this truly acute thinker that if all things fall downwards in straight lines, no atom would ever overtake another, and so he availed himself of a pure fiction. He said that the atom swerves slightly from its path (a most ridiculous suggestion), and that this leads to combinations, aggregations, and adhesions of atoms, which, in their turn, lead to the formation of a world' (*De Natura Deorum*, i. 69).

THE NATURE OF REALITY

The *infinite worlds.*—The Epicurean definition of a 'world,' or orderly system of atoms, is 'a region of the heavens, containing stars, an earth, and all perceptible bodies, cut off from the void and terminated by a boundary which may be in rotation or at rest, and may have a round, a triangular, or any other figure. For all figures are possible, since no evidence can be found to the contrary in our own world, since its boundary is not perceptible' ([*Ep.*] ii., Usener, p. 37). In this definition the words 'cut off—void' are known to be a quotation from Leucippus, and what precedes them probably comes from the same source; the addition that such a 'world' may or may not be moving as a whole, and may have any shape, is partly at least original, since it alludes to the peculiar Epicurean theory of knowledge. Epicurus also borrows from Leucippus and Democritus the doctrine that the universe contains an infinite number of such worlds. 'We see that the number of such worlds is infinite, and that such a world may arise either within another world, or in the intermundial spaces, by which we mean the intervals of empty space between different worlds.' As we have seen, Epicurus maintained that any number of divergent explanations of the formation of the things composing a world might be equally good, provided that they only exclude all divine agency and conform to the general principles of atomism. Of the movements of the heavenly bodies it is expressly said, 'To assign one single explanation of these facts when

69

the phenomena suggest several is the action of a
lunatic, and a very improper proceeding of those who
emulate the follies of the astronomers' (*i.e.* the scientific
astronomers of the Platonic school). He even scandalised the scientific by the ridiculous assertion that
the heavenly bodies are approximately of their apparent
size. 'Relatively to us the size of the sun and moon
and the other heavenly bodies is just what it appears
to be; absolutely it is either a little larger or a little
smaller, or as the case may be.' His argument is that
a bonfire seen from a distance appears about as big as
it really is, and we may conclude to the case of the
sun and moon by analogy. So generally we find the
'second letter' full of alternative explanations of facts
in which the results of the latest science and the crudest
guesses of the earliest Milesians are treated as much on
a par.

I do not propose to enter here into the details of
these ludicrous theories, but there is one point on
which a word should be said. The Epicureans have
sometimes been unduly belauded as pioneers of the
doctrine of 'evolution.' In point of fact, the general
conception of the origin of species by gradual development is as old as Anaximander of Miletus in the early
part of the sixth century, and had been specially
expounded by Empedocles in the fifth. Hence, as
there is, so far as I know, no evidence that Epicurus
concerned himself much with the subject, I think it
most probable that the remarkable anticipations of

Lamarck which we find in the fifth book of Lucretius come from Empedocles, whom he regarded as his literary model, rather than from Epicurus. The real way to put the matter is that Epicurus, like the evolutionists, rejects all teleological explanation of natural facts. Eyes and ears have not been 'given to us,' as Plato had asserted, in order to lead us to philosophic reflection and scientific knowledge. We do not have eyes and ears that we may see and hear; we see and hear merely because we happen to have eyes and ears. Function does not create organisation, as modern biologists are teaching us; organs create function.

Psychology.—The soul is, of course, material and made of atoms. The only immaterial existent is empty space, but empty space cannot act or be acted on as the soul can. 'Hence those who call the soul immaterial talk nonsense. If it were so, it could neither act nor be acted upon. But in fact it is clear and evident that both these states belong to the soul' (*Ep.* i., Usener, p. 21). More particularly, it is made of the finest and roundest particles, and this accounts for its quickness of sensibility and volition, such particles being more mobile than any others. (This is merely Democritus repeated.) 'We can see by appealing to sensation and feeling, the surest of criteria, that the soul is a subtle body scattered through our whole frame, similar to breath, with an admixture of warmth, and that in some parts it is more like the one, in some like the other, but in one special part [I read ἐπὶ δέ του μέρους for Usener's ἐπὶ δὲ τοῦ μ., which may be an oversight,] it far surpasses even breath and heat themselves in fineness, and is consequently all the quicker to be affected by the condition of the rest of our frame' (*Ep.* i., Usener, pp. 19-20). According to the still more precise account followed by Lucretius (iii. 227 ff.) and the *Placita* of Aëtius (iv. 3, 11), the soul is 'a mixture of four things, one of a fiery nature, another of the nature of air, a third of the nature of breath, and a fourth which has no name. It is this last which is the sensitive principle; the "breath" is the source of motion, the "air" of rest, the hot element of the sensible heat of the body, while the nameless principle produces sensation in us, for there is no sensibility in any of the elements which have got names.'

It is this fourth 'nameless' part which Lucretius regularly calls the *anima* (mind), as distinct from the *animus* or soul as a whole. Thus to the other three constituents Epicurus assigns the functions of respiration, motion, and the like. They constitute the vital principle; the unnamed fourth part is the principle of sensation, and, since all mental activity is based on sensation, of consciousness generally. We have to think of the soul as not localised in any one part of the body but diffused through it, particles of the soul-stuff being everywhere mixed up with the grosser particles which form the 'flesh,' as Epicurus prefers

to call the body. But *consciousness* is more definitely
located in a special region, that of the heart, since the
atoms of the 'nameless part' are held to be con-
gregated there. The difference between the soul and
the body thus becomes one of degree. The soul is no
longer, as with Plato, different in kind from and in-
commensurable with the body, nor, as with Aristotle,
the true reality of which the body is the mere indispensable condition. As with Democritus, the soul is
itself a body composed of smaller and more mobile
atoms than the gross visible body. Sensation and all
the other mental processes are thought of as actual
movements belonging partly to the 'flesh,' partly to
the soul. The bodies of the outer world are always
shedding off skins or coats of surface-atoms, which for
a while cohere and retain the shape of the body from
which they are emitted. And, in course of time, some
of these atoms may be dissociated from their original
setting and joined with others to form a new skin or
image. When a 'husk' of either of these kinds comes
in contact with a sense-organ, it may literally force a
passage through into the organism. If it can hang
together until it reaches the 'nameless' part of the
soul and impinges on it, there arises a conscious
sensation. This theory of sensation as due to the
actual entrance of atomic 'skins' into the body comes
from Democritus, except that, whereas Democritus had
supposed the 'skins' to be formed out of the air or
water which surrounds bodies, and to be propagated

73

through air or water to the percipient, Epicurus holds that they are formed of atoms actually detached from the perceived body itself, and propagated through empty space with an infinite velocity. The whole theory, of course, ignores the fundamental fact of which a doctrine of perception has to take account, the personal individuality of the perceiving self.

Since the soul is formed of the smallest and most mobile atoms, it would naturally be more quickly dissipated into its constituents than anything else in Nature, if it were not that it is shielded during life by the integument of grosser atoms which surrounds it. Thus it is not the soul which holds the body together, but the body which holds the soul together. Hence, at death, when the soul is eliminated from its covering, the body, it is instantly disintegrated, and consciousness and personality are finally annihilated. 'When the whole complex is dissolved, the soul is dispersed and no longer has the same powers, no longer is moved nor has perception. For that which perceives can no longer perceive anything, since it no longer belongs to this complex nor has these motions, since the things which envelope and surround it are not such as those in which it now exists and possesses these motions' (*Ep.* i., Usener, p. 21). The ethical inference is then drawn that it is folly to fear death, since there is no consciousness after death. 'Death is nothing to us, for when we are, death is not; and when death is, we are not.'

'Accustom thyself to reflect that death is nothing to us, since good and bad depend entirely on sensation, and death is privation of sensation. Hence the true knowledge that death is nothing to us makes mortal life enjoyable, not by adding endless duration to it, but by taking away the craving for immortality. There is nothing terrible in life for one who really comprehends that there is nothing terrible in not living. Hence he who says he fears death, not because it will be painful when it comes, but because our present assurance that it will come is painful, is a fool. It is but an idle pain that comes of anticipating a thing which will give us no uneasiness when it has come. Death, then, that most dreaded of ills, is nothing to us. For while we are, death is not; and when death has come, we are not. Death, then, is nothing to the living nor yet to the dead, since it does not affect the former, and the latter no longer exist. The crowd, to be sure, at one time shrink from death as the worst of evils, at another choose it as a refuge from the miseries of life. But the wise man neither declines life nor shrinks from death, since life is not distasteful to him, nor does he think it an evil not to live' (*Ep.* iii., Usener, p. 60). Thus Epicurus uses his borrowed Psychology to achieve the extirpation of the fear of death as a prime disturber of human happiness.[1]

---

[1] The famous dilemma, 'Death cannot concern us, for so long as we are, death is not, and when death is, we are not,' seems

EPICURUS

Theology.—The climax of the Epicurean Physics is
to be found in its theory of the gods, which, by cutting
them adrift altogether from human life, rids us of all
fear of their anger or anxious concern to win their
approval.   Epicurus and his followers were often
denounced as Atheists, and the accusation is just if
it means that they denied the existence of gods from
whom we have anything to hope or fear, gods who
can be objects of our love or can help humanity in its
hour of need.   They admit the existence of gods in
the sense of superhuman beings who lead a life of
unending blessed calm.   They even insist on their
existence and anthropomorphic character.   Epicurus
himself in his letter to Menoeceus has the words,
'Follow and dwell on what I used constantly to
declare to you, and believe that these things are the
foundation of a worthy life.   Believe, in the first
place, of God that he is an imperishable and blessed
living being, as the universally diffused idea of God
testifies, and ascribe to him nothing inconsistent with
his immortality nor unworthy of his blessedness.   But

to be no more original than the rest of Epicurus' philosophy.
The pseudo-Platonic dialogue *Axiochus* (a polemic against
Epicurus by a contemporary Platonist) asserts that the words
were a saying of Prodicus the sophist, and the statement may
very possibly be true, since the author's aim is to show that
Epicureanism, which he describes as the superficial talk of
conceited young men, is merely a reproduction of the discredited ideas of an older time.   Unless the saying really came
from Prodicus, he has made a literary blunder in putting it
into his mouth in such a connection.

believe everything which can consist with his immortal blessedness. For gods there certainly are, since our cognition of them is clear and evident. But gods such as the vulgar believe in there are not. . . . The impious man is not he who rejects the gods of the vulgar, but he who ascribes to the gods the things which the vulgar believe of them.'

The Epicurean gods are thus thought of as magnified and 'non-natural' Epicurean philosophers, enjoying, like the Epicurean sage, a life of perfect tranquillity, with the added advantage of being immortal. They are human in figure and there are many of them, so that they can pass their time in pleasant social intercourse. Epicurus is said to have declared that in their converse they speak the noblest of languages, a pure and refined Greek. There is an obvious difficulty about their immortality for expositors who take Epicurus seriously as a thinker. For they are material, like everything except space itself, and Epicurus explicitly declared that their bodies are formed of the subtlest matter. How then do they escape the general law that all atomic complexes are destructible, and the finer the atoms, the less permanent the complex? It is partly, no doubt, to meet this difficulty that Epicurus provided them with abodes in the intermundial empty spaces, where they would be least subject to collision with grosser atoms. At least Lucretius gives this reason for the localisation.

Now Epicurus held that tranquillity is only possible

to one who is neither anxious for others nor gives others anxiety. Hence it is a consequence of the felicity of the gods that they neither influence earthly affairs by their providential care, nor concern themselves with the deeds of men. This is laid down in the very first words of the *Catechism*: 'The blessed and immortal has no anxieties of its own, and causes none to others. Thus it is constrained neither by favour nor by anger.' Lucretius is constantly recurring to the same point with an earnestness which shows that the inherently anti-religious doctrine of Epicurus was, in his case at least, accepted in part from a real religious indignation against the immoral features of popular theology. Yet one wonders whether the amiable invalids of the garden would not have been seriously perturbed in their 'feasts on the 20th' by the apparition of a disciple aflame with the zeal of a missionary. I cannot help thinking that Epicurus would have given his worshipper the counsel of Voltaire, *Surtout point de zèle*. The moral fervour of Lucretius must not blind us to the facts that he stands alone among the Epicureans of whom we know, and that the real issue at stake in the Academic polemic against Epicurus is the momentous one whether or not religion shall continue to be of practical significance for life. Yet in justice to Epicurus it may be said that, after all, his rejection of Providence and prayer leads to something not unlike the Neo-Kantian view that while we cannot know whether God exists or not, the concept of God is none the less valuable as embodying an ethical ideal of perfection. The gods of Epicurus are, at least, an embodiment of the ideal ' wise man,' and thus the contemplation of them may be of actual use in framing one's own mind to something like their peace and serenity. This is, perhaps, why Epicurus speaks of the thought of the gods as bringing the greatest benefits to the good.

CHAPTER III

THE SALVATION OF MAN

WE come now to the central citadel of Epicurean
doctrine, the part which, as Epicurus holds, gives all
the rest its value—the theory of human conduct,
variously styled by him the doctrine of *Lives*, of *Ends*,
of *Choice and Avoidance*. Here again we shall find the
attempt to replace high and difficult ideals by some
more homely and apparently more easily compassed
end of action. Epicurus wants a principle of conduct
which is not for the elect few only, but can be
immediately understood and felt by the common man.
Like many moralists before and after him, he thinks
he finds what he wants in the notion of pleasure as
the only good and pain as the only evil. The Platonic
conception of life as 'becoming like unto God,' the
Aristotelian identification of the best life with one in
which, by means of science, art, religious contemplation, we put off the burden of our mortality, may be
inspiring to the chosen few, but to the plain average
man these are noble but shadowy ideas. And for
what is shadowy the prosaic Epicurus has no taste.
'The consecration and the poet's dream' are to him

empty nothings. 'I call men,' he writes in one letter, 'to continual pleasures, not to empty and idle virtues which have but a confused expectation of fruit' (*Fr.* 116); and in another place, 'I spit on the noble and its idle admirers, when it contains no element of pleasure' (*Fr.* 512). But pleasure and pain are things we all know by immediate experience, and what could seem a simpler basis for conduct than the rule that pleasure is good and pain bad? So Epicurus seeks once more to bring down moral philosophy from heaven to earth by reverting to Hedonism. The naturalness of the view that pleasure is the only ultimate good, says Epicurus, borrowing an argument from Plato's pupil Eudoxus, is shown by the spontaneity with which all animals seek it. 'His proof that pleasure is the end is that animals delight in it from their birth and object to pain spontaneously, independently of any process of education.' Like other Hedonists, he has been roundly abused for degrading morality by his doctrine, but some of the abuse at least may be pronounced undeserved. When we consider how many philosophies and religions have done their best to make life miserable by representing the tormenting of ourselves and others as admirable in itself, we may feel that some credit is owing to any man who is not afraid to maintain that happiness is itself a good thing, and that to be happy is itself a virtue. And, as we shall see, Epicurus does not in the least mean that the best life is that of the voluptuary. He taught and enforced by his example the doctrine that the simple life of plain fare and serious contemplation is the true life of pleasure, and in the main, with one great exception, the practical code of action he recommends does not differ much from that of the ordinary decent man. The main objection to his Hedonism is a theoretical one; as he regards the feeling of pleasure as the only good, he is bound to deny that virtue or beauty has any moral value except as a necessary means to pleasure, and thus his ethics, while demanding an innocent and harmless life, can afford no inspiration to vigorous pursuit of Truth or Beauty, or strenuous devotion to the social improvement of man's estate. The air of the Garden is relaxing; it is a forest of Arden where nothing more is required than to 'fleet the time carelessly.' There is a touch of moral invalidism about the personality of a teacher who could declare that 'the noble, the virtuous, and the like should be prized if they cause pleasure; if they do not, they should be left alone' (*Fr.* 70). To be more precise, in saying that pleasure is the good, Epicurus is not telling us anything new. Hedonism as a moral theory is dealt with in Plato's *Protagoras,* had been advocated by Democritus, and expressly put forward within the Academy itself by Eudoxus.[1]

What does look at first sight more original is the

[1] It is usual at this point to bring the Cyrenaic school into the story as precursors of the Hedonism of Epicurus. This is, however, historically wrong. The ancient do not appear to

way in which Epicurus conceives of the highest pleasure
attainable by man. He holds the curious view that,
though pleasure is a positive thing not to be con-
founded with mere absence of pain, yet the moment
pain is entirely expelled from the mind and body we
have already attained the maximum degree of pleasure.
Any further increase in the pleasure-giving stimulus,
according to Epicurus, can only make pleasure more
variegated, not increase its intensity. 'The (upper)
limit of pleasures in magnitude is the expulsion of
all pain. Where pleasure is present, and so long
as it is present, pain and grief are, singly and con-
jointly, non-existent' (*Catechism*, § 3). 'Pleasure
receives no further augmentation in the flesh after
the pain of want has once been expelled; it admits
merely of variegation' (*ib.* 18). The source of this
pessimistic estimate of the possibilities of pleasure
is patent; the doctrine comes from Plato's *Philebus*.
Plato had taught that the satisfactions of appetite are

have known of a Cyrenaic doctrine before the time of the
younger Aristippus; and in Plutarch, *Adv. Colotem*, we find
Arcesilaus and the Cyrenaics specifically contrasted with Plato,
Aristotle, Stilpo, and Theophrastus as the *contemporaries* of
Colotes. This, presumably, like most of the statements in
Plutarch's anti-Epicurean essays, goes back to a much earlier
Academic source (very possibly Carneades), and is therefore
not likely to be a misapprehension. The earlier philosophers
who have influenced Epicurus in his theory of the end are
demonstrably Democritus and Eudoxus. It was exactly the
same blunder in chronology which long led scholars to suppose
that the anti-Hedonist polemic of Plato's *Philebus* was aimed
at the Cyrenaics.

never purely pleasurable; they are 'mixed' states, half-pleasurable, half-painful. They depend for their pleasantness upon a pre-existing painful state of want, and the process of satisfaction only continues so long as the pain of the want is not completely assuaged, but still remains in the total experience as a stimulus to go on seeking more and more satisfaction. The 'true' pleasures—*i.e.* those which do not depend for their attractiveness on the concealed sting of unsatisfied want —belong to the mind, not to the body. It is to meet this depreciation of the everyday pleasures of satisfying bodily appetite that Epicurus declares the complete expulsion of pain and want to be already the maximum attainable degree of pleasure, and denies the existence of the 'mixed' experiences. The *alma voluptas* of his school thus comes to mean a life of permanent bodily and mental tranquillity, free from disquieting sensations and from the anticipation of them—a view which he has merely taken over from Democritus, who spoke of εὐθυμία, 'cheerfulness of temper,' as the true end of life. What he has done is simply to express the Democritean theory in a terminology specially intended to mark dissent from the Platonic and Aristotelian doctrine. His own words are: 'The end of all our actions is to be free from pain and apprehension. When once this happens to us, the tempest in the soul becomes a calm, and the organism no longer needs to make progress to anything which it lacks, or to seek anything further to complete the good for soul and body. For we only need pleasure so long as the absence of it causes pain. As soon as we cease to be in pain we have no need of further pleasure. This is why we call pleasure the beginning and end of the happy life. It is recognised by us as our primal and connatural good, and is the original source of all choice and avoidance, and we revert to it when we make feeling the universal standard of good. [*Eudoxus.*] Now it is *because* this is our primal and connatural good that we do not choose to have every pleasure, but sometimes pass by many pleasures when a greater inconvenience follows from them, and prefer many pains to pleasures when a greater pleasure follows from endurance of the pain. Every pleasure then is a good, as it has the specific character of the good [*i.e.* to attract us for its own sake], but not every pleasure is to be chosen; so also every pain is an evil, but not every pain should be always avoided' (*Ep.* iii., p. 62, Usener). Hence he differs from his Cyrenaic contemporaries, who preached a robuster type of Hedonism, in three points. (1) The *end* of the individual action is not the pleasure of the *moment*, but a permanent lifelong condition of serene happiness. So, unlike Aristippus, he does not accept the doctrine of taking no thought for the morrow, but says 'we must remember that the future is neither wholly our own, nor wholly not our own, that we may neither await it as certain to be, nor despair of it as certain not to be' (*Ep.* iii., Usener, p. 62). (2) Epicurus insists strongly that pleasures are not all 'transitions' from one condition to another; besides the pleasures of transition there are καταστηματικαὶ ἡδοναί, pleasures of repose, a point which had already been made by Plato and Aristotle. He says: 'Freedom from mental disquietude and from pain are pleasures of repose; joy and delight we regard as activities of change' (*Fr.* 2). Hence he is often wrongly classed among those who regard *mere* freedom from pain as the highest good. (3) He definitely gives the preference to pleasures of mind over pleasures of body, arguing that 'in bodily pain the flesh is tormented merely by the present, but in mental pain the soul is distressed on account of the present, the past, and the future. Similarly mental pleasures are greater than bodily' (*Fr.* 452). They are greater, that is, because they include the memory of past and the anticipation of future happiness. Indeed, Epicurus carried this doctrine to the point of paradox, saying that a 'sage' would be happy on the rack, since his pleasant recollections of the past would outweigh his bodily sufferings (*Fr.* 601). Later writers like Seneca are never tired of making merry over the Epicurean 'sage' who must be able to say, even while he is being roasted alive, 'How delightful this is! How I am enjoying myself!' Epicurus, as we have seen, illustrated the doctrine practically by the serenity of his last painful days. But, as the Academic critics are careful to remind us, we must recollect that all the mental pleasures of memory and anticipation, to

which Epicurus attributes such value, are resoluble
into the recollection or anticipation of pleasurable experiences which are themselves analysable into sensations, and therefore corporeal.

As we should expect, Epicurus is never tired of
denouncing all ascetic views about the pleasures of
bodily appetite. He insists *ad nauseam* that man has
a body as well as a soul, and that the happy life is
impossible if we neglect the claims of the body. He
and his friends often put the point in coarse and
vigorous language, which scandalised persons of
refined turn of mind. Metrodorus said in a letter to
his brother Timocrates, 'The doctrine of nature is
wholly concerned with the belly' (*Fr.* 39), and
Epicurus that 'the beginning and root of all good
is the pleasure of the belly, and even wisdom and
culture depend on that' (*Fr.* 67). Metrodorus, probably using a formula devised by his master, asks
'what else is the good of the soul but a permanent
healthy condition of the flesh, and a confident expectation of its continuance?' (*Fr.* 5), a definition which is
a perpetual subject for denunciation by the Academic
critics. The real meaning of sayings like these is more
innocent than it looks to be. Epicurus is, after all,
only saying in exaggerated language, that even a
philosopher cannot afford to neglect his digestion.
The fact that both he and Metrodorus were confirmed
dyspeptics goes far to explain the vehemence of their
language about the 'pleasures of the belly.' Carlyle

might easily have said the same sort of thing, and Dr. Johnson, who was far from being a voluptuary, actually did.

More open to attack was Epicurus' trick of abstracting from the whole concrete experience of the satis-factions of virtuous action, and asserting that the pleasure which accompanies the right act is the end to which the act itself is merely a means. This leads him to the utilitarian view that if you could only escape the painful consequences which attend on indulgence in a pleasant vice, the vice would no longer be bad. 'If the things which give rise to the pleasures of the profligate could deliver our under-standing from its fears about celestial portents, and death, and future suffering, and could also teach us to limit our desires, we should have no reason left to blame them' (§ 10 of the *Catechism*). This is, of course, a conscious contradiction of the famous Platonic doctrine, that to have a bad soul is itself the worst penalty of sin. Epicurus, however, holds that this separation of vice from its attendant consequences is not actually possible. The pleasures of sin are always attended by the fear of detection and punishment, and often by other disagreeable consequences. Also they cannot teach us to limit our desires, and thus escape the torment of unsatisfied passion. Nor can they, like science, dispel the fear of death or divine judgment. This, and not any inherent badness in them, is why they must not be admitted into our lives. The true conditions of a happy life are two : (1) the assurance that all consciousness ends with death, and that God takes no interest in our doings ; (2) the reduction of our desires to those which cannot be suppressed and are most easily satisfied ; the simple life. Epicurus accordingly recognises that there are three classes of pleasures : (1) those which are natural and necessary, *i.e.* those which come from the satisfaction of wants inseparable from life, such as the pleasure of drinking when thirsty ; (2) those which are natural but not necessary, *e.g.* the pleasures of a variegated diet, which merely diversify the satisfaction of our natural appetites ; (3) those which are neither necessary nor natural, but created by human vanity, such as the pleasure of receiving marks of popular esteem, 'crowns' and 'garlands,'—as we might say, knighthoods and illuminated addresses. The wise man despises the last class, he needs the first, the second he will enjoy on occasion, but will train himself to be content without them. (The basis of this classification is Plato's distinction, in the *Philebus*, between 'necessary' and 'unnecessary' bodily pleasures. The sensualism of Epicurus compels him to take no account of Plato's 'pure' or 'unmixed' pleasures, such as those which arise from the performance of noble deeds, or the pursuit of beauty and truth for their own sakes.)

Epicurus, then, looks on the simple diet not as necessary in itself to happiness, but as useful by keeping us from feeling the lack of delicacies which cannot be procured. 'We regard self-sufficiency as a great good, not that we may live sparingly in all circumstances, but that when we cannot have many good things we may be content with the few we have, in the fixed conviction that those who feel the least need of abundance get the greatest enjoyment out of it' (*Ep.* iii., Usener, p. 63). Thus in practice the Epicurean ideal comes to be satisfaction with the simplest necessaries of life, and Epicurus could say (*Catechism,* § 15), 'natural riches are limited in extent and easy to procure, while those of empty fancy are indefinite in their compass'; and again (*Fr.* 602), 'give me plain water and a loaf of barley-bread, and I will dispute the prize of happiness with Zeus himself.' So enemies of the theories of the school often praise its practical counsels. As Seneca says, 'my own judgment, however distasteful it may be to the adherents of our school [*i.e.* the Stoics], is that the rules of Epicurus are virtuous and right, and, on a clear view, almost austere; he reduces pleasure to a small and slender compass, and the very rule we prescribe to virtue he prescribes to pleasure; he bids it *follow Nature.*' Even of the tortures of disease he holds that they cannot disturb true happiness. If severe, they are brief; if prolonged, they are interrupted by intervals of relief.

In practice, then, though not in theory, Epicurus refuses to separate pleasure and virtue. 'You cannot live pleasantly without living wisely and nobly and justly, nor can you live wisely and nobly and justly without living pleasantly. Where any one of these conditions is absent pleasurable life is impossible' (*Catechism*, § 5).

In respect of the details of his scheme of virtues, Epicurus is enough of a true Greek to give the first place to φρόνησις, *wisdom*, *reasonable* life. 'He who says that it is not yet time for Philosophy, or that the time for it has gone by, is like one who should say that the season for happiness has not yet come, or is over. So Philosophy should be followed by young and old alike: by the old that in their age they may still be young in good things, through grateful memory of the past; by the young that they may be old in their youth in their freedom from fear of the future' (*Ep.* iii., ·Usener, p. 59). 'When we say that pleasure is the end, we do not mean the pleasures of the profligate, nor those which depend on sensual indulgence, as some ignorant or malicious misrepresenters suppose, but freedom from bodily pain and mental unrest. For it is not drinking and continual junketing, nor the enjoyments of sex, nor of the delicacies of the table which make life happy, but sober reasoning which searches into the grounds of all choice and avoidance, and banishes the beliefs which, more than anything else, bring disquiet into the soul. And of all this the foundation and chiefest good is wisdom. Wisdom is even more precious than Philosophy herself; and is the mother of all other intellectual excellences' (*Ep.* iii., Usener, p. 64).

EPICURUS

Of all the fruits of Philosophy the chief is the acquisition of true friendship. 'Of all that Philosophy furnishes towards the blessedness of our whole life far the greatest thing is the acquisition of friendship' (*Catechism*, § 27). The solitary life is for Epicurus, as for Aristotle, no life for a man who means to be happy. He would have agreed with some recent writers that the highest good we know is to be found in personal affection. We have already seen how closely analogous the Epicurean organisation, bound together by no tie but the personal affection of its members, was to the early Christian Church, in which also love for the brethren replaces the old Hellenic devotion to the 'city' as the principle of social unity. Hence it is not surprising that Epicurus, like Our Lord, is credited with the saying that it is more blessed to give than to receive. In his attitude towards the State Epicurus naturally represents a view antithetic to that of Plato and Aristotle, who insisted upon common service to the 'city' as the basis of all social virtue. Unlike Aristotle, who teaches that man is by his very constitution a 'political animal,' a being born to find his highest good in the common life provided by the community into which he comes at birth, Epicurus revives the old sophistic distinction between the 'natural' and the 'conventional,' taking the purely conventional view as to the origin of political society and the validity of its laws. Societies are merely institutions created by compacts

92

devised by men to secure themselves against the in-
conveniences of mutual aggression. 'Natural justice,'
he says, 'is an agreement based on common interest
neither to injure nor to be injured.' 'Injustice is not
an evil in itself, but because of the fear caused by
uncertainty whether we shall escape detection by the
authorities appointed to punish such things.' 'It is
impossible for one who has secretly done something
which men have agreed to avoid, with a view to
escaping the infliction or reception of hurt, to be sure
that he will not be found out even if he should have
gone undetected ten thousand times' (*Catechism*,
§§ 31, 34, 35).

Law, then, has no deeper foundation in human
nature than agreement based on considerations of
utility. It is only when such an agreement has been
made that an act becomes unjust. Hence Epicurus
holds that brutes have no rights because, from
their lack of language, they can make no agreements
with one another. The personal friendship of the
'brethren' is a thing which goes infinitely deeper and
is more firmly rooted in the bed-rock of human nature,
though even friendship is held to be founded in the
end on mere utility. Of Plato's conception of law as
the expression of the most intimately human, and, at
the same time, the most divine element in our
personality, Epicurus has no comprehension. So
though his doctrine, as preserved in the *Catechism*,
is that the 'wise man' will in general conform to the

laws, since some of them are obviously based on sound utilitarian considerations, and even the breaking of those that are not is likely to have unpleasant consequences, Epicurus definitely refuses to say that the wise man will never commit a crime. His words, as reported by Plutarch, are: 'Will the wise man ever do what the laws forbid, if he is sure not to be found out? It is not easy to give an unequivocal answer to the question.' Plutarch interprets this to mean, 'He will commit a crime if it brings him pleasure, but I do not like to say so openly.' It must be allowed that on Epicurus' own showing his 'wise man' would have no motive for refraining from a pleasant crime if he really could be secure of impunity. The 'sage' is not a person whom one would care to trust with the 'ring of Gyges.'

It was a consequence as much of the age as of the Epicurean ideal that Epicurus dissuaded his followers from taking part in public life. They were to leave the world to get on by itself, and devote themselves to the cultivation of their own peace of soul by plain living and anti-religious reasoning. This separation of personal conduct from service to society is the point on which the Epicureans lay themselves most open to attack as representing an ethics of selfishness and indolence. We may plead in palliation that their 'quietism' may be regarded as partly a necessary consequence of the substitution of large monarchies for the old city states. In such monarchies, even when

their code of public morality does not keep men of
sensitive conscience out of public life, it is inevitable
that the direction of affairs of moment shall be confined
to a few practised hands. Yet it must also be re-
membered that not a few philosophers, Academics,
Stoics and others did play a prominent part in the
public affairs of the age without soiling their garments.
It is impossible to acquit Epicurus and his friends
altogether of a pitiable lack of wholesome public
spirit. It was only reasonable that a noble temper
like that of Plutarch should be outraged by the
insults they heaped on the memory of such a states-
man and patriot as Epameinondas because he preferred
wearing himself out in the service of his country to
taking his ease at home. In practice, however, as the
ancient critics observed, the apparently contradictory
maxims of Epicurus and Zeno were not so far apart
as they seem. Epicurus said that the 'sage' should
not engage in politics except for very pressing reasons;
Zeno that he should, unless there were special reasons
against doing so. But in actual life an Epicurean with
a bent for politics, or a Stoic with a taste for retire-
ment, could always find that the reason for making the
exception existed in his own case.

By following the rules of life thus laid down the
Epicureans hold that any man, without need of special
good fortune or high station or intellectual gifts, may
learn to lead a life which is free from serious pain of
body or trouble of mind, and therefore happy. The

'sober reasoning' which teaches him to limit his wants to the necessities of life, to banish fear of God from his mind, to recognise that death is no evil, and to choose always the course of action which promises to be most fruitful of pleasure and least productive of pain, will, in general, leave him with very few pains to endure. And if there are inevitable hours of suffering to be gone through, and if death is the common doom of all, the 'wise man' will fortify himself in his times of suffering and on his deathbed by dwelling in memory on the many pleasant moments which have fallen to his share. Thus prepared, says Lucretius, he will leave the feast of life, when his time comes to go, like a guest who has eaten his full at a public banquet, and makes way without a grumble for later comers; Metrodorus adds, that he will not forget to say 'grace after meat,' and thank 'whatever gods there be' that he has lived so well (*Fr.* 49).

CHAPTER IV

EPICURUS AND HIS CRITICS

WE have already had a glimpse into the polemics waged incessantly by Epicurus and his friends against the adherents of all views but their own, and have made aquaintance with some of the 'Billingsgate' employed by Epicurus to disparage those who ventured to differ from him or had the misfortune to have taught him something. The first school to take up the battle for the 'religious' view of the world against the new secularism of Epicurus was the Platonic Academy. Their polemic against the 'Garden' began, as we shall see, with the definitive settlement of Epicurus at Athens, and was steadily kept up until, in the third and fourth centuries after Christ, as it became more and more clear that the Christian Church was putting itself forward as a rival to Philosophy, the various schools became gradually merged into the Neo-Platonism which represents the last gallant struggle of Greek culture against what was felt as largely a non-Hellenic and ominous invasion of Orientalism. We can form a very fair conception of the way in which the controversy was carried on from the Academic

side, if we compare the dialogue *Axiochus*, falsely attributed to Plato, with the tone of the Academic anti-
Epicurean speakers in Cicero (such as *e.g.* Cicero
himself in the examination of the Epicurean ethics
given in *De Finibus* Bk. II., or Gaius Cotta in the polemic of *De Natura Deorum*, against their theology), and
with the utterances of the biting essays in which
Plutarch has set himself to demolish the philosophical
reputation of Colotes. In particular the very close
correspondence between Cicero and Plutarch, often
amounting to verbal self-sameness, shows that both are
following the same Academic source (in all probability
Cleitomachus, the pupil who preserved for later generations the penetrating inquiries of Carneades, the Hume
of the ancient world). As the *Axiochus* and the essays
of Plutarch against Colotes are much less widely read
than the *De Finibus* and *De Natura Deorum* of Cicero,
I shall probably provide the more entertainment for
the reader by confining my concluding remarks chiefly
to the former. The *Axiochus* is a singularly interesting
specimen of a third-century 'Socratic discourse.' There
can be no doubt about the date at which it was written,
since it expressly alludes to the Epicurean argument
that death is no evil, because it is mere unconsciousness, and, neither good nor evil is possible without
consciousness, as the 'superficial talk' which is for the
moment popular with the young, and its language is
full of biting sarcasms, the point of which lies in
turning specially Epicurean dicta against Epicurus

himself. Thus the date of the little work cannot be
earlier than 306 B.C.—the year of Epicurus' final settlement in Athens—and cannot again be much later, since
as Otto Immisch, the one recent editor of the dialogue
and the first student to recognise its real purpose, has
pointed out, there are several indications in the con-
versation that Epicurus had not yet broken with his
Democritean teachers or with the pursuit of rhetoric
so completely as he did in later life. The dialogue is
thus definitely to be dated at about forty years after
the death of Plato, but its preservation in Platonic
manuscripts means, of course, that it comes from the
archives of the Academy, and is therefore a genuine
Academic composition. At the time to which we must
attribute it the most famous members of the School
were Polemon, the fourth head of the Academy, Crates,
Crantor, and Arcesilaus, afterwards famous for his
brilliant dialectical criticism of Stoicism. Of its authorship we have no precise indication beyond the fact that
the writer must have been an enthusiast for astronomy,
and writes in a turgid style full of violent metaphor and
poetical reminiscences. Immisch, its last editor, thinks
of Crantor, whose essay on Bereavement, famous in later
antiquity, was imitated in the lost *Consolatio* addressed
to himself by Cicero, on the death of his daughter, as
well as in the extant *Consolatio* to Apollonius ascribed
to Plutarch. But the identification, as Immisch says,
is the purest guess. Whoever the writer may have
been, it is interesting to observe that the fashion of

99

composing 'discourses of Socrates' was still current in
the Platonic school a century after Socrates' death.
That the dialogue was not a work of Plato was well-
known to the ancient critics who included it with
a few others in the list of those 'universally
rejected.'

The plan of the little work is transparently simple.
Socrates is called in to administer spiritual consolation
to his old friend Axiochus, who has just been attacked
by what appears to be a kind of epileptic fit, and is in
a pitiable condition of mental weakness. He had
formerly been in the habit of deriding the cowardice
of those who shrink from death, but now that he is face
to face with the prospect of dissolution his courage has
oozed out of him. He dreads the approaching loss of
the good things of life, and shudders at the thought of
worms and corruption and the ugliness of the fate
which awaits his body.

Socrates at first ironically puts on the mask of an
Epicurean, and, in language which is filled with
Epicurean terminology, adroitly employed in such
a way as to insinuate that Epicurus is no more
than a charlatan who has dressed up the exploded
theories of fifth-century 'sophistry' in a rhetorical garb
suited to the taste of the young generation, 'consoles'
Axiochus by the usual Epicurean commonplaces.
Death is utter unconsciousness, and therefore all
suffering ends in death; it is 'nothing to us, because,
so long as we are, death is not, and when death has

come, we are not.' These well-meant efforts at consolation prove a failure; as Axiochus says, discourse
of this kind sounds very fine while you are well and
strong, but when you come to face death on a sick-bed,
there is nothing in it which can take hold of the heart.
Socrates then suddenly drops the mask, and appears
as a convinced Platonist. He dwells on the blessed
immortality which awaits the soul after its release
from its earthly prison, and enforces his doctrine in
true Socratic style, by an Orphic myth, setting forth
the joys of heaven, the perpetual banquet (the
'marriage-supper of the Lamb'), the angelic harpings
and hallelujahs, the trees bearing all manner of fruit,
the water of life, the unending raptures of worship.
Axiochus finds himself not merely reconciled to his
fate, but already 'half in love' with death. Thus the
main object of the author is to urge that the Epicureans
can provide only a spurious remedy for the fear of
death; the real cure for it is to be sought in just those
beliefs which Epicurus forbids us to entertain, faith in
God as the righteous judge of spirits, and in the
glorious immortality which awaits the 'saints.' One
or two points of this anti-Epicurean polemic call for
special notice. The writer makes it specially clear
that one of his chief charges against Epicurus is his
entire want of originality, thus striking a note which
persists throughout the whole controversy between the
two schools from first to last. Just as Cicero's Academic
speakers insist on the point that the Physics of Epicurus

is no more than a bad echo of the doctrine of Democritus, the writer of the *Axiochus* lays special emphasis
on the assertion that the famous arguments which
were to banish the fear of death are mere borrowings
from the supposed wisdom of Prodicus. Indeed, he
goes further and seems to insinuate that Epicurus has
borrowed these arguments from a professed pessimist
without seeing that they are inseparable from a pessimistic theory of life quite incompatible with the
Epicurean views as to the happiness of the 'wise man.'
For Axiochus makes a remark which is obviously very
pertinent, but to which the Epicurean theory hardly
admits of any reply. The familiar argument about
the absurdity of thinking that any evil can befall us
when we have ceased to be may be valid enough.
But if death is the end of all, we may reasonably shrink
from it, not as the beginning of the unknown, but as
the end of all the known good things of life. Epicurus
has really no answer to this but to revile the greed of
those who make such complaints; but Socrates is
ready with a reply which he professes to have got, like
the rest of his wisdom, from the discourses of Prodicus. It is not true that death is the end of the good
things of life, because life is actually evil. There is
no age of man, and no profession or calling, in which
the inevitable pains are not many and great, while
the incidental pleasures are few and fleeting. Death
therefore should be doubly welcome, since it not only
sets us free from all apprehensions for the future, but

delivers us from the miseries of the present. The obvious, and as it seems to me, the correct implication is that in Epicurus we have an illogical combination of Hedonism with a view of death which is only in place in the mouth of a professed pessimist. Equally interesting is another point to which Immisch has rightly called attention. In the 'Platonic' discourse of Socrates on the hope of immortality we find, besides the Orphic myth of judgment and Paradise, great stress laid on two thoughts. Man's superiority to the rest of the creation and his destination to a life beyond the grave are suggested (1) by the record of his rise from barbarism to civilisation and (2) by his success in reading the secret of the movements of the heavenly bodies. He can 'despise the violence of mighty beasts, make his way over the seas, build cities to dwell in, establish governments, look up to the heavens, behold the circuits of the stars and the course of moon and sun,' etc. All this he could never have done 'if there were not indeed the breath of God in his soul.' The first part of this argument is directed against the Epicurean doctrine of human progress as a sort of unintentional by-product of an accumulation of slight advances in the adaptation of the organism to its environment, each motivated by considerations of immediate utility. Epicurus, in fact, thought of man as merely an animal among others, endowed with an inexplicable superiority in taking advantage of favourable variations and learning by his past mistakes. 'We must suppose that Nature herself learns and is constrained to many things of many kinds in the course of events themselves, and that reflection afterwards takes over what is thus handed down to it by Nature and puts a further finish on it, and makes further discoveries' (*Ep.* i., Usener, p. 26-7, with which we may compare the account of human progress in Lucretius, v. 925 and what follows). The Platonist argument against Epicurus, which is identical in spirit with T. H. Green's argument against the 'naturalism' of Spencer and Lewes, is that this very tendency to progress bears witness to a 'divine' or 'spiritual' principle in man.

The argument from astronomy (the supreme veneration for this science is a genuine Platonic touch, and comes from the *Laws* and *Epinomis*) is, in a like way, specially aimed at the characteristic Epicurean conception of the part played by Physics in effecting a happy life. The whole value of Physics for Epicurus lies in the supposed fact that it expels God's Providence and moral government from the universe, just as Nietzsche has said that the great service of Physics is to have *proved* the non-existence of God. The Platonist rejoinder is that Physics is, indeed, entitled to the highest honour, but for the very opposite reason, that 'the heavens declare the glory of God,' and the ability to read their lessons testifies to the presence of the 'godlike' in human nature. Thus, as Immisch puts it, we may fairly say that the real issue at stake in the controversy of the Academy with Epicurus, an issue raised in the *Axiochus* and never afterwards lost sight of, is the perennial conflict between a purely secular and a religious conception of the world and our place in it. Hence it is not surprising that the main arguments by which the Platonists support their views are exactly the same as would now be urged by Christians in the controversy with secularism. Little has changed in the conflict except the names adopted by the contending parties; the two rival interpretations of life and the world remain in principle the same. This comes out most clearly of all in the *Essays* of Plutarch against the Epicurean doctrine. We have already seen some of the reasons for thinking that the basis of Plutarch's attacks, as well as that of Cicero's, goes back as far as Carneades, the great Academic opponent of dogmatic empiricism in the second century B.C. But there are at least two features of Plutarch's work which seem to belong to the man himself: the intense warmth of personal religious feeling, and the local Boeotian patriotism which pervade it. Plutarch's chief contribution to the controversy consists of two essays more specially directed against the early Epicurean Colotes. Of the man himself we know little more than a single anecdote which is a source of standing delight to the ancient critics of the 'mutual admirationism' of the Epicurean coterie. He joined the school in its early days at Lampsacus, and signalised his 'conversion' by publicly

'venerating' Épicurus as a god at the end of one of
his discourses on Physics. Epicurus returned the
compliment by 'venerating' Colotes and calling him
'immortal.' This may have been meant as a piece of
good-natured satire on the extravagance of Colotes,
but the Academic writers prefer to take the performance more seriously, and make merry over the
disappointment of Colotes at finding himself promoted
only to the rank of a 'hero.' Colotes wrote a work
with the title 'That life itself is an impossibility on
the principles of the other philosophers,' in which he
caricatured and abused impartially all philosophies
except that of Epicurus. Plutarch's two essays take
the form of an examination and refutation of this work.

The essay 'against Colotes,' which is largely concerned with Colotes' attack on the distinctive tenets
of the rival schools, need receive no attention here.
The other essay, which exhibits the Academic criticism
of Epicurean ethics at its best, bears a title happily
parodied from that of the book of Colotes itself, 'That
happy life is impossible on the principles of Epicurus';
the very suggestion which had already been made in
the *Axiochus*. I propose to conclude this short account
with a very brief summary of this acute and penetrating
attack on secularistic Hedonism.

The author begins by defining the precise position
he intends to sustain. All questions about the moral
value of the Epicurean life are, for the time, to be
set aside; the case for or against Epicurus is to be

argued on strictly Hedonist lines. He and Colotes profess to regard pleasure as the good. We will not, in the first instance, ask whether this is or is not a satisfactory theory. Our question is whether, admitting pleasure to be the good, the Epicurean life affords the best way to secure the most of it. It is then argued (*a*) that the doctors of the sect expressly hold that the primary sources of pleasure and pain are bodily. It is on the pleasures and pains of the body that the whole superstructure of the mental happiness of memory and anticipation is based. As to this we may remark that bodily pleasures are dependent on the activity of a few specialised organs ; pain, and that in the most cruel forms, may attack any and every part of the body. Bodily pleasures, again, are brief thrills which come and go like meteors ; bodily pain, set up in one part, may spread itself to others and so come to persist for seasons and even years together. As far as the body is concerned, it must be pronounced that its pleasures are as nothing to the pains to which it is exposed. But (*b*) the Epicureans themselves profess that purely bodily pleasures do not count for much ; they rest their case on the pleasures of the mind, which, they say, can persist under the direst bodily tortures. Now on this we may remark that if bodily pain is as trifling a thing as Epicurus often declares it to be, and if also, as he asserts, you at once enjoy the maximum possible pleasure the moment you cease to be in pain, the pleasures which reach their highest intensity as soon as pain is expelled must also be very petty things. But we may meet them with an argument which goes much more deeply into the psychology of the School. According to their own doctrine, the contents of the mind are mere paler after-effects of actual sensation. Memory-images are washed-out and blunted sensations, and we may liken the pleasure which they awaken, in comparison with the pleasure accompanying actual sensation, to the scent left behind in an emptied wine-bottle. A 'wise man' who tries to make himself happy by imaginatively dwelling on the details of past sensual enjoyments is like a man who tries to banquet on the stale remains of yesterday's feast. Epicurus, in fact, plays a game of 'hanky-panky' with his disciples. He tells you that the pleasures which are to outweigh all the pains of life are those of the soul; but when you ask what are the pleasures of the soul they turn out to be only a feebler mental survival of those of the body. Now our bodily frame is so much the sport of circumstance and accident that its 'servility to all the skiey influences' is a commonplace of literature, and this simple fact makes nonsense of the identification of the good with 'an equilibrium of the flesh conjoined with a confident anticipation of its continuance.' The 'equilibrium' is, in the first place, difficult of establishment and brief in duration, and, in the second place, its continuance, in a world fraught with such dangers as ours, can never be counted on. Thus the ideal of Epicurus and

Metrodorus is that of fools. Mere freedom from pain and anxiety is not the good, but merely the 'necessary,' an indispensable condition of the attainment of something better, but of no value in itself. (c) And not only is the Epicurean good notoriously unobtainable, but it carefully omits all those pleasures which decent men judge to be the worthiest. Their account of the mental pleasures leaves no room for any except those which accompany, or are fainter reinstatements of, a somatic 'thrill.' Hence they cannot recognise (1) the pleasures of literature and science (in fact Epicurus notoriously tried to keep his young friends from devoting themselves to either), (2) nor those which accompany a life well-spent in the service of the community. In fact, though they use the most extravagant language about the superhuman virtue of an Epicurean who has rendered some very trifling service to a friend, they have nothing but raillery and abuse for the lives of the great statesmen and soldiers who have been the common benefactors of civilisation. In a word, they leave out of their computation of pleasures all those which make life worth living to any one but a moral invalid.

The argument next proceeds to examine the claim of Epicurus to have made life infinitely more pleasurable by freeing mankind from the fear of God and the dread of hell. Plutarch goes on to give a very interesting account of the effects of religious convictions on human happiness, which ought to be carefully pondered before we make any assertion on the vexed question how far ancient Greek life was really over-shadowed, as Epicurus and Lucretius assume it to have been, by terrors of this kind. His view is that Epicurus has absurdly overrated the extent to which theological beliefs cause unhappiness. That they do so sometimes he allows, but urges that they give rise to an overwhelmingly greater amount of happiness. We may divide mankind, he says, into three classes. (1) There is the small 'criminal' class. Their belief in God and the future must, no doubt, give rise to fear, pure and simple. But it is well that they should be thus afraid, not merely on the ground of public safety, but because, so far as their fear of God's judgments restrains them from actually committing projected crime, it makes them better men by saving them from guilt. Epicurus would be doing a very bad service even to the habitual criminal himself, if he could persuade him that the 'last things' are mere fables. (2) There is the very large class of mostly decent, but philosophically uninstructed persons. With them the thought of God is tempered with fear (they show this by that scrupulous anxiety to discharge the ceremonial obligations of religion which the Greeks called *deisidaimonia*), but fear is not the dominant note. Their belief in God as the giver of all good is merely qualified by an undertone of salutary fear. Attendance on the ceremonies of worship is in the main a source of pleasure to them, because they feel themselves in the presence of wise and kindly powers. Even to the day-labourer and the drudge religion is a boon with its holidays and feast-days. And the rich, who can fare sumptuously every day, are happiest of all when they celebrate the feasts of religion, not because they are faring better than usual, but because they feel the presence of God. A man who denies Providence cuts himself off from all this happiness. He may share in the ritual, but it can give no joy to him, since he looks on it all the while as a mummery. (3) Finally there are the few 'philosophers' who have really enlightened views about God and the relation of God to man. To them religion is a source of unalloyed delight; there is no trace of fear in their feelings towards God, since they know Him to be perfectly good, and the author of nothing but good, the 'giver of all good things' (Zeus Epidotes), 'the God of all consolation' (Zeus Meilichios), the 'defender of all that put their trust in Him' (Alexikakos). 'All things are God's, and they are the friends of God, and therefore all things are theirs.' Epicurus' treatment of immortality receives a similar criticism. The fear of hell is positively good for the criminal class. As for the mass of decent men, when they think of the life to come, they feel no fear of 'bogies' who have often been paraded on the comic stage for their amusement. Immortality is a thought which fills them with happiness; it offers a satisfaction for the 'longing to go on living' which is natural to us all;

or if the ordinary man is, now and then, disconcerted
by the old wives' tales, there are cheap and innocent
religious rites which will restore his equanimity.
What he really does shrink from is the very prospect
which Epicurus holds out as the greatest boon,
annihilation. To be always harping on the thought
that 'we have been born as men once; there is no
second birth, and we shall never be again to all eternity'
is to 'die many times before our death.' As for the
real children of God, immortality means for them the
'prize' of their calling, the beholding of the beatific
vision face to face, and the reunion with their loved
ones who have gone before. Even descending from this
high strain, we may say that the belief that death is
the gateway to a better life adds to the joys of the
fortunate and consoles the unfortunate by the thought
that their ill-luck here is no more than a troublesome
accident on a journey which has home for its goal.
On the Epicurean view, death is an evil to fortunate
and unfortunate alike; it is the end of the good things
of life to the one class, the end of all hope of a change
for the better to the other. The wisdom of Epicurus
is thus the merest foolishness. At best it enables a
man with difficulty to argue himself into a state into
which a brute is born. It is better to be a pig than
an Epicurean philosopher, for the pig neither takes
thought for the morrow nor fears God nor distresses
himself about death and what comes after death; and
as for the 'equilibrium of the flesh,' it is as much his,

if he is a fairly healthy pig, as the philosopher's. And what better good does the Epicurean buy at the price of his everlasting poring over his master's precepts?

If human nature is much the same in all ages, one would suppose that Plutarch's account of the attitude of mankind to Theism and Immortality in the ancient world is much nearer the truth than that of Epicurus. One might almost fancy that when he 'went round with his mother, reading spells for her,' he had imbibed childish terrors from which he had never been able to shake himself free. The pathological character of Lucretius' horrors of the world to come is sufficiently marked for us by the intensity of imagination with which he depicts them. Yet there were, in later ages, men who seem, without the need of salvation from such morbid fears, to have found real consolation in this uninspiring theology. Lucian seems to speak from his heart when he says with reference to the burning of Epicurus' *Catechism* by the impostor Alexander, 'How little the wretch knew how great good that little book does to those who fall in with it, what peace, what calm, what freedom of soul it effects in them; how it rids them of terrors and hobgoblins and bugbears, and extravagant and idle fancies; how it fills them with truth and reason, and purifies their judgments in very deed, not by torches and squills or any such impostures, but by sound discourse, and truth, and frank speaking.' Even more touching is

the summary of Epicurean teaching which Diogenes
of Oenoanda in Pisidia, a schoolmaster of the early
Imperial time, inscribed on the walls of the little town
in order that the words which had brought peace and
happiness into his own life might remain after his
death for the spiritual benefit of his townsmen and of
any chance visitors whose eyes they might catch.

APPENDIX

If you would make Pythocles rich, seek not to add to his possessions but to take away from his desires. (Epicurus to Idomeneus, Us., Fr. 135.)

You must be the slave of Philosophy if you would attain true freedom.   (Seneca, *Ep. Mor.*, 8. 7.)

If you make nature the rule of your life, you will never be poor, if current opinion, you will never be rich.   (*Ib.*, 16. 7.)

He who follows nature and not empty opinions is content in any estate, for, measured by the standard of what is enough for nature, any property is wealth; but measuring by our unlimited appetites, even the greatest wealth is poverty.   (Us., Fr. 202.)

We have been born once; there is no second birth. For all time to come we shall not be at all.   Yet, though you have no power over the morrow, you put

115

off the season [*i.e.* for acquiring Philosophy]. It is this procrastination that ruins the life of us all; thanks to it each of us dies without tasting true leisure. (Us., Fr. 204.)

In all things act as though the eye of Epicurus were on you. (Seneca, *Ep. Mor.* 25. 5.)

Severe pain soon makes an end of us, protracted pain has no severity. (Us., Fr. 447.)

Let us give thanks to our lady Nature that she has made things needful easy to procure, and things hard to procure needless. (*Ib.*, Fr. 468.)

He who least craves for the morrow will go to meet it most happily. (*Ib.*, Fr. 490.)

Laws are made for the sake of the wise, not to prevent them from inflicting wrong but to save them from suffering it. (*Ib.*, Fr. 530.)

We can provide ourselves with defences against all things but death; where death is concerned, all mankind are dwellers in an unfortified city. (Metrodorus, Fr. 51. The saying is also ascribed to Epicurus.)

We should not esteem a grey-beard happy because he dies in advanced age, but because he has had his fill of good things; in respect of *time*, we are all cut off in our flower. (Metrodorus, Fr. 52.)

There are some who spend a life-time in preparing to live, as though they were to have a second life after what we call 'life.' They do not see that the draught of birth poured out for each of us is a deadly poison. (*Ib.*, Fr. 53. The first sentence is also attributed to Antiphon the Sophist. Metrodorus must have the merit of the piquant metaphor.)

Only the 'wise man' knows how to show himself grateful. (*Ib.*, Fr. 54 ; from Seneca, *Ep. Mor.* 81. 11.)

He who wastes his youth on high feeding, on wine, on women, forgets that he is like a man who wears out his overcoat in the summer. (*Ib.*, Fr. 55.)

If we do not repay the loan of life quickly, Nature comes down on us like a petty Shylock and takes eyesight or hearing, or often enough both, as pledges for the settlement. ([Plato] *Axiochus*, 367 B ; clearly another of the picturesque Epicurean metaphors.)

Cheerfulness on a couch of straw is better than a golden couch and a sumptuous table, and disquiet of mind therewithal. (Epicurus, Fr. 207.)

Retire most of all into thyself when thou art forced to be in a crowd. (*Ib.*, Fr. 208.)

EPICURUS

Nothing novel can happen in a universe which has already existed through infinite time.   (Epicurus, Fr. 266.)

If God heard men's prayers, mankind would have perished long ago, for they are ever invoking cruel curses on one another.   (*Ib.*, Fr. 388.)

A CHRONOLOGICAL TABLE USEFUL TO THE READER OF THIS BOOK

	B.C.
Plato dies, and is succeeded by Speusippus, .	347
Epicurus born in Samos, 7th Gamelion, . .	341
Speusippus succeeded by Xenocrates, .	339
Aristotle opens his School in Athens, . .	335
Stilpo of Megara 'flourishes,' . . .	c. 330
Death of Aristotle at Chalcis; Theophrastus head of the Lyceum, ...	322
Expulsion of Athenian settlers from Samos, .	322
Timon the Sillographer born, . . .	315
Xenocrates dies ; Polemo head of Academy, .	314
Epicurus collects disciples at Mytilene and Lampsacus, ...	c. 310
Epicurus established at Athens . . .	306-5
Stoic School founded by Zeno of Cittium, .	c. 300
Theophrastus dies ; Strato head of Lyceum, .	287
Metrodorus dies (Arcesilaus head of Academy about this time), ...	276
Epicurus dies, . . .	270
Antigonus of Carystus 'flourishes,' . . .	c. 250 (?)
Carneades born, ...	213
Sotion of Alexandria writes his 'Successions,' .	c. 200
Chronica of Apollodorus first published, .	144
Carneades dies, ...	129

EPICURUS

	B.C.
Lucretius born, . . .	99
Cicero attends the Lectures of Phaedrus at the age of nineteen, ...	88
Cicero hears Phaedrus and Zeno of Sidon at Athens,	79
Death of Lucretius, ...	55
Philodemus at Rome, . . .	c. 52

(Date of Cicero's attack on Piso)

	B.C.
Cicero writes the *De Finibus*, . . .	45
Cicero writes *De Natura Deorum*, . . .	44

	A.D.
Seneca writes his *Epistulae Morales*, . .	59-65
Plutarch 'flourishes,' . .	68-125
Lucian 'flourishes,'	c. 160
Sextus Empiricus 'flourishes,' . . .	c. 200
Inscription of Diogenes of Oenoanda,	c. 200

or a few years earlier.

A SHORT LIST OF BOOKS USEFUL TO THE ENGLISH STUDENT OF EPICURUS

[Works on Ancient Philosophy or on Ancient Atomism in general are excluded, as are also works dealing specially with the exposition of Lucretius.]

I. Sources. *Epicurea* ; edidit Hermannus Usener. Leipzig, Teubner, 1887. (Anastatic reprint, 1903.) A complete critical text of all the remains of Epicurus known up to 1887, with (Latin) Prolegomena on their authenticity, the form in which the Epicurean correspondence circulated in antiquity, etc. Indispensable to serious study.

Metrodori Epicurei Fragmenta. Edited by A. Koerte. Leipzig, Teubner, 1890.

Lucretius de Rerum Natura. Text, translation, and commentary. H. A. J. Munro. Fourth edition. Cambridge. Deighton, Bell & Co., 1893. (Translation obtainable separately, as a volume of Routledge's New Universal Library.)

Diogenes of Oenoanda. Ed. J. William. Leipzig, B. G. Teubner, 1907.

PLUTARCH. The Essays against Colotes will be found in vol. 6 of *Plutarchi Moralia.* Ed. G. N. Bernardakis. Leipzig. B. G. Teubner, 1888-1896.

CICERO. *De Finibus Bonorum et Malorum.* Ed. Madvig, Copenhagen, 1869 (2nd ed.).

—— *De Natura Deorum.* Ed. J. B. Mayor. 3 vols. Cambridge, 1880.

EPICURUS

PHILODEMUS. *Rhetorica.* (2 vols. with supplement.) Ed. S. Sudhaus. Leipzig, Teubner.

II. WALLACE, WILLIAM. *Epicureanism.* London, Society for Promoting Christian Knowledge, 1880. (A specially fascinating introduction to the study of the Epicurean doctrine and its fortunes.)

HICKS, R. D. *Stoic and Epicurean.* New York, 1910. Charles Scribner's Sons. (A volume in the recently projected series, *Epochs of Philosophy*, edited by J. G. Hibben.)

GUYAU, JEAN MARIE. *La Morale d'Épicure.* Paris, 1878.

And as a standard work for reference,

ZELLER, E. *The Stoics, Epicureans and Sceptics.* Translated (from the author's great work *Die Philosophie der Griechen*) by O. J. Reichel. London, Longmans, Green & Co. (The latest edition of the relevant part of the original German work is *Philosophie der Griechen*, iii. 1. 4th edition. Leipzig, 1909.)

See also the fuller Bibliography in the work of R. D. Hicks, mentioned above.

Printed by A. Constable Printer to His Majesty
at Edinburgh University Press

Lightning Source UK Ltd.
Milton Keynes UK
UKOW06f2035120913

217112UK00007B/286/P

9 781178 245370